THE GLORY DUE HIS NAME
WHAT GOD SAYS ABOUT WORSHIP

GARY REIMERS

BOB JONES
UNIVERSITY PRESS

Greenville, South Carolina

Library of Congress Cataloging-in-Publication Data

Reimers, Gary R., 1955–
  The glory due His name : what God says about worship / Gary R. Reimers.
    p. cm.
  Includes bibliographical references.
  Summary: "Explains what the Bible teaches about worship"—Provided by publisher.
  ISBN 978-1-60682-025-4 (perfect bound pbk. : alk. paper)
  1. Worship—Biblical teaching. I. Title.
  BS680.W78R45 2009
  248.3—dc22
                              2009021340

BWHEBB [Hebrew] and BWGRKL [Greek] Postscript® Type 1 and TrueTypeT fonts Copyright © 1994–2006 BibleWorks, LLC. All rights reserved. These Biblical Greek and Hebrew fonts are used with permission and are from BibleWorks, software for Biblical exegesis and research.

All Scripture is quoted from the Authorized King James Version unless otherwise noted.

ESV: Scripture quotations marked ESV are from The Holy Bible, English Standard Version®, copyright © 2001 by Crossway Bibles, a publishing ministry of Good News Publishers. Used by permission. All rights reserved. **HCSB**: Scripture quotations marked HCSB are taken from the Holman Christian Standard Bible®, Copyright © 1999, 2000, 2002, 2003 by Holman Bible Publishers. Used by permission. Holman Christian Standard Bible®, Holman CSB®, and HCSB® are federally registered trademarks of Holman Bible Publishers. **NASB**: Scripture quotations marked NASB taken from the NEW AMERICAN STANDARD BIBLE®, Copyright © 1960, 1962, 1963, 1968, 1971, 1972, 1973, 1975, 1977, 1995 by The Lockman Foundation. Used by permission. **NEB**: Scripture marked NEB taken from The New English Bible. © 1970 by Oxford University Press and Cambridge University Press. **NET**: Scripture quoted by permission. Quotations designated (NET) are from the NET Bible® copyright ©1996-2006 by Biblical Studies Press, L.L.C. www.bible.org/. All rights reserved. This material is available in its entirety as a free download or online web use at http://www.nextbible.org/. **NIV**: Scripture marked NIV taken from the HOLY BIBLE, NEW INTERNATIONAL VERSION®. Copyright © 1973, 1978, 1984 by International Bible Society. Used by permission of Zondervan Publishing House. All rights reserved. **NKJV**: Scripture taken from the New King James Version. Copyright © 1982 by Thomas Nelson, Inc. Used by permission. All rights reserved. **NLT**: Scripture quotations are taken from the Holy Bible, New Living Translation, copyright 1996, 2004. Used by permission of Tyndale House Publishers, Inc., Wheaton, Illinois 60189. All rights reserved. **NRSV**: The scripture quotations marked NRSV herein are from the New Revised Standard Version of the Bible, copyright 1989, by the Division of Christian Education of the National Council of Churches. Used by permission. All rights reserved.

The Glory Due His Name: What God Says About Worship
Gary Reimers, PhD

Design and page layout by Nathan Hutcheon

© 2009 by BJU Press
Greenville, South Carolina 29614
Bob Jones University Press is a division of BJU Press

Printed in the United States of America
All rights reserved

ISBN 978-1-60682-025-4

15 14 13 12 11 10 9 8 7 6 5 4 3 2

*To the two churches that have granted me
the opportunity to serve as pastor:
Heritage Baptist Church, Dover, New Hampshire (1983–1998)
Cornerstone Baptist Church, Greenville, South Carolina (2002–present).
It has been a privilege to pursue biblical worship together.*

Contents

Preface vii

Introduction 1

1 True Worship's Essence and Elements 4

2 Multi-Generational Impact:
  Worship Style and Your Family 51

3 The Dangers of Deviant Worship 70

Conclusion 98

PREFACE

Faithful Christians in every generation hunger for *Biblical Discernment for Difficult Issues*, the title of this book series authored by the faculty of Bob Jones University Seminary. The true disciple thirsts for a life that reflects Christ's love for others while striving to maintain loyalty to God's revealed Truth, the Scriptures. But as every mature Christian soon learns, demonstrating both God's compassion and God's holiness in this life is a balance that is never easy to strike.

Our propensity to wander from the right path is enough to alarm any honest follower of Christ. How quickly in our pursuit of holiness we do race into the darkness of a harsh, unforgiving condemnation of others who somehow lack the light we enjoy. And how tragically inclined we all are to slip, while on the narrow way, from the firm ground of genuine compassion into the mire of an unbiblical naiveté or an unwise sentimentality. Only by God's grace can the believer combine that loving compassion and that pursuit of a rigorous holiness into one life to bring the true "light of the knowledge of the glory of God in the face of Jesus Christ" to a needy church and a lost world.

The aim of this series is to provide help in finding this right, discerning balance in spiritual life without sacrificing one crucial emphasis in Scripture for another. While written in an easy-to-read style, these works attempt to combine mature, penetrating theological thought with thorough research. They aim to provide both a fact-intensive exposition of Scripture and a piercing application of it to real human experience. Hopefully those who read will find themselves making significant strides forward on the way to a renewed mind and a transformed life for the glory of Christ.

Stephen J. Hankins, Dean

Bob Jones University Seminary

INTRODUCTION

Matthew closes his Gospel with the Great Commission, but his transition to this final topic is puzzling. "Then the eleven disciples went away into Galilee, into a mountain where Jesus had appointed them. And when they saw him, they worshipped him: but some doubted" (Matt. 28:16–17). The reader is optimistic after the triumphant climax of the resurrection account, and the picture of the disciples worshiping the Lord on a mountaintop is climactic and heartwarming. Matthew adds three words, however, that leave us somewhat puzzled: "But some doubted." Surely this does not indicate continued unbelief about the reality of Christ's resurrection; the appearances on two successive Sundays in the upper room in Jerusalem had settled that issue (John 20:19–29). Matthew is indicating that some other problem exists among Christ's followers. Although scholars have struggled with this verse, most agree that the verb refers not to unbelief but to hesitation.[1]

---

[1]See Craig Blomberg, *Matthew*, in New American Commentary (Nashville: Broadman & Holman, 1992), 340. Leon Morris suggests that it is not the Eleven who hesitated but a larger crowd (even though Matthew does not mention any other people). *The Gospel According to Matthew* (Grand Rapids: Eerdmans, 1992), 744–45. D. A. Carson declares that none of the proposed interpretations he has encountered is convincing, concluding, "We are left with some uncertainty about what Matthew means." "Matthew," in *Expositor's Bible Commentary*, ed. Frank E. Gaebelein (Grand Rapids: Zondervan, 1984), 8:593–94. Donald Hagner, however, demonstrates that Matthew's use of οἱ δὲ elsewhere indicates that all eleven disciples are included in the action of the following verb. (The article functions as a pronoun.) *Matthew 14–28*, in Word Biblical Commentary (Dallas: Word, 1995), 884. John Nolland suggests that οἱ δὲ refers to the eleven plus the larger group of followers that included the women. *The Gospel of Matthew*, in the New International Greek Testament Commentary (Grand Rapids: Eerdmans, 2005), 1262.

This hesitation seems to relate directly to their worship. The disciples know who the Lord is and instinctively bow to give Him glory, but their efforts somehow fall short. This may be exactly Matthew's point: in spite of Who He is and what He has done, Jesus Christ is receiving inadequate worship.[2] In fact, Matthew has hinted at two problems with worship: the quantity of disciples is insufficient (only eleven), and the quality of disciples is insufficient (they hesitate). The seriousness of these deficiencies becomes clear in verse 18 when Matthew quotes Christ's rightful claim that He has been put in charge of everything in the universe. There is no one more powerful or more important than He is. No one is more worthy of worship. The Lord deserves better worship than He is currently receiving.

My first serious concern with the deficiencies of worship came while writing my doctoral dissertation.[3] The topic was not directly related to worship, but it required spending much time studying and researching the second commandment and its consequent corollaries (Exod. 20:4–6), which are all about worship. Shortly after that project, I planted a new church in a small New England city. The responsibility of leading other people in worship caused me to think more deeply about the biblical basis for what we were doing. Then God began to bless our home with children, and the role of fatherhood added another level of responsibility as I led my own family in worship. These factors and others drove me to the Scriptures for information and convictions about what God desires and

---

[2]Blomberg (340) offers what may be the most likely explanation: "They may simply continue to exhibit an understandable confusion about how to behave in the presence of a supernaturally manifested, exalted, and holy being." That is a confusion disciples today continue to exhibit.

[3]Gary R. Reimers, "The Significance of the Visitation of the Sins of Fathers on Children for the Doctrine of Imputation" (PhD diss., Bob Jones University, 1984).

demands from those who worship Him. The following pages are the result of that study.

Biblical worship, of course, is not limited to one hour or so on the Lord's Day. Private worship and public worship are mutually dependent activities. Private worship occurs on two levels. First, everything that a believer does should honor the Lord, down to the most mundane activities. As Paul says in 1 Corinthians 10:31, "Whether therefore ye eat, or drink, or whatsoever ye do, do all to the glory of God." In that sense worship is a 24/7 activity. On another level, however, private worship is a special daily event when the individual believer focuses on the Lord and devotes himself to Him.[4] Public worship, then, should involve people who have individually committed themselves to honoring the Lord and serving Him each day. They gather together in a joint expression of God's worthiness. As such, the public worship service is the glorious culmination of everything that has preceded. It is not only the highlight of the week, it is the highlight of life itself. At the same time, public worship occurs at the beginning of the week (the "first day," 1 Cor. 16:2),[5] marking the starting point that sets the standard for all that follows. Private worship is essential and requires careful attention, but this study will focus on public worship as the necessary first step in a life that strives to "do all to the glory of God."

---

[4]Donald S. Whitney identifies the first level as a more indirect form of worship: "There is a sense in which all things done in obedience to the Lord, even everyday things at work and at home, are acts of worship." *Spiritual Disciplines for the Christian Life* (Colorado Springs: NavPress, 1991), 88. He also describes the key element of the second level: "So no matter what you are saying or singing or doing at any moment, you are worshiping God only when you are focused on Him and thinking of Him" (89).

[5]David E. Garland explains that the first day "refers to the Christians' day of worship in commemoration of the resurrection. Paul appears to avoid the heathen term 'Sunday.' On the 'first day' Christians gather for the breaking of bread to honor the Lord (Acts 20:7) and to remember the sacrifice of their Lord." *1 Corinthians*, Baker Exegetical Commentary on the New Testament (Grand Rapids: Baker, 2003), 753.

1

TRUE WORSHIP'S ESSENCE AND ELEMENTS

There is a story about a young apprentice who was serving under a respected sculptor. The young man marveled at the skill of his mentor. Although he was learning much, he still believed that he was missing something very important. One day as the master finished a beautiful sculpture of an angel, the young apprentice could contain himself no longer. "How do you do that?" he exclaimed. The master smiled and said, "It is not very complicated. I just chip away anything that is not an angel. Perhaps you are ready to try." He gave the eager student a large block of marble and left him alone. When the master returned, he gasped at what he saw: on the table was a tiny piece of shapeless stone, with little chips covering the floor. After an awkward silence he asked quietly, "What happened?" "Well," the young man began, not sure how to answer, "I tried to do what you said. I chipped away everything that wasn't an angel, but I don't think there was an angel in this one!"

There is an important parallel to worship. People often assume that worship is easy and takes place automatically whenever they go to church. In fact, they hardly give worship any thought at all. As we will see in chapter 3, Scripture has provided sufficient examples of wrong worship for us to know what God does not want us to do. Eliminating what is wrong, however, might leave nothing of value that could make our worship pleasing to God. It is necessary to add in what is right, and for that we must turn to God's Word.

THE ESSENCE OF RIGHT WORSHIP

One of the greatest blessings of studying worship in the Bible is also one of the greatest challenges: there are a great many passages to consider. Indeed, the entire book of Psalms is itself a major worship primer. Many themes, of course, show up repeatedly, but the volume of material can be daunting. A complete biblical theology of worship, then, is well beyond the scope of this short discussion. Instead, the goal here is to present the key principles that form the heart of true worship, using the passages of Scripture that reflect those principles most clearly.

Right Worship Must Focus on the Right Person (Psalm 135:1–6)

In recent years some churches have grown to ten thousand people or more in a relatively short time. One pastor explained the rapid growth of his church this way: "People are coming to our worship services because we give them what they want." Is there something wrong with that statement? Is it possible that churches are designing their worship services with the focus on the wrong person? Psalm 135:1–2, like so many other psalms, calls upon all God's people to adopt a singular focus on the Lord:

> Praise ye the Lord. Praise ye the name of the Lord; praise him, O ye servants of the Lord. Ye that stand in the house of the Lord, in the courts of the house of our God.[1]

Worship is an event where God should be the center of attention and the guest of honor. To accomplish that goal, churches should be designing their worship services with the focus on Him. The

---

[1] H. C. Leupold suggests that those who "stand in the house of the Lord" could be limited to temple officials or could include all who come to worship. *Exposition of the Psalms* (Grand Rapids: Baker, 1959), 924. Derek Kidner, on the other hand, is confident that the psalm "has a great and varied throng in view, priestly and lay." *Psalms 73–150*, in The Tyndale Old Testament Commentaries (Downers Grove: InterVarsity, 1975), 455.

book of Revelation portrays the perfected worship of heaven, with the Lord on His throne at the center of concentric circles of worshipers (4:4, 6). The theme of their praise is that the Lord is "worthy to receive glory and honour and power" (11). The similarity between the words *worship* and *worthy* is not circumstantial. Long ago the English language used to spell the word *worship* as "worthship," denoting the process of ascribing worth to a deity. Worship, then, should point to the Lord as worthy, which is what they do in heaven. Imagine an angel turning to one of the twenty-four elders in Revelation 4 to ask if there was anything they should change about the worship service that would make him feel more special. Why does that question seem any less ludicrous for a worship service on earth?

A clear focus on God should highlight aspects of His character and activities that deserve praise.[2] That is why Psalm 135 goes on to provide two main reasons why the focus should be on God alone: because He is good (3–4), and because He is great (5–6):

> Praise the Lord; for the Lord is good: sing praises unto his name; for it is pleasant. For the Lord hath chosen Jacob unto himself, and Israel for his peculiar treasure. For I know that the Lord is great, and that our Lord is above all gods. Whatsoever the Lord pleased, that did he in heaven, and in earth, in the seas, and all deep places.

God continually demonstrates His goodness through His provision and protection as well as countless other blessings. High on that list is the blessing that has made us recipients of His goodness: He has chosen us to be His people, much as He chose the

---

[2]As Donald Whitney observes, "The more we focus on God, the more we understand and appreciate how worthy He is. As we understand and appreciate this, we can't help but respond to Him." *Spiritual Disciplines*, 87. Michael P. V. Barrett adds, with simple profundity: "God deserves worship because of who He is." *The Beauty of Holiness* (Greenville, SC: Ambassador International, 2006), 61.

people of Israel. That is a good reason to focus our worship on Him. In addition, the psalmist points to God's greatness. He is exalted above all other gods, and He exercises complete sovereignty over the entire universe. The list of God's attributes that deserve worship is long, as is the list of instances of His goodness. God's people should delight to reflect upon them all, each in turn, leading to a genuine response of worship.

Right Worship Must Accomplish the Right Purpose (Psalm 96:7–8)

Before one can accomplish the purpose of worship, he must identify that purpose. Probably every book on this topic has included a definition of worship. Some come from the dictionary, but most derive from one or more key passages of Scripture.[3] The goal of such a definition is to express in a succinct statement what worship is all about. It should provide clear direction about what God expects us to do. I believe we find such a definition in Psalm 96:7–8:

> Give unto the Lord, O ye kindreds of the people,
>
> give unto the Lord glory and strength.
>
> Give unto the Lord the glory due unto his name:
>
> bring an offering, and come into his courts.

These two verses present an emphasis that would be hard to miss. In four slightly different ways this passage says just one thing: worship is giving God glory.[4] A question arises immediately: how

---

[3]Andrew E. Hill does both: "One may always consult *Webster's Dictionary* for the precise meaning of worship (adore, idolize, esteem worthy, reverence, homage, etc.). Yet truly defining worship proves more difficult because it is both an attitude and an act." *Baker's Theological Dictionary of the Bible*, ed. Walter A. Elwell (Grand Rapids: Baker, 1996), 837. He then goes on to present a commendable survey of the subject.

[4]Ryken arrives at the same definition from a different passage: Colossians 3:16–17. *City on a Hill* (Chicago: Moody, 2003), 63.

can people give God *anything*, much less glory? The dilemma, of course, is that God already has everything He needs, and we have nothing of value to give. Clearly worship cannot actually contribute anything to God, but it can attribute something to him. Many modern translations clarify the issue by translating the imperative verb with the word *ascribe* instead of *give*.[5] Worship, then, is the process of declaring, by whatever means God ordains, that the Lord is full of glory.

This all seems simple enough, but there is often a disconnection between theological apprehension and practical application. One could look at the statement *worship is giving God glory* and ask, "Who doesn't know that?" Indeed, it seems to be needless to say. On the other hand, if we ask, "Who doesn't do that?" the answer may well be self-incriminating. At this point we come face to face with a major presupposition among God's people: they return from a church service assuming that they have successfully fulfilled the responsibilities of worship. But have they?

For years I have posed the following scenario to both students in seminary classrooms and people in church pews. Imagine you are listening to the conversation in the family car on the drive home after a Sunday morning worship service. One of the parents glances back toward the children occupying the rear seats and tries to prompt a positive evaluation of the morning activities by asking, "Did you get anything out of the service today?" After a thoughtful pause the response may be something like this: "Well, yes, we sang one of my favorite hymns today, so I really enjoyed that. The choir sounded good, too." Then, picking up the level of enthusiasm a bit, he adds, "And the pastor preached on the same

---

[5]See, for example, the ESV, NASB, NIV, HCSB, NRSV, and NET Bible. The NKJV, of course, retains the word *give*, while the NLT has *recognize* in verse 7 (twice) and *give* in verse 8. All of the above have *bring* in the fourth line.

topic that we studied in Sunday school, so that was cool." Hearing that, the parents nod toward each other with satisfaction.

Did you discern what was wrong with that picture? The answers were all positive and encouraging (on that day, at least!). The problem is not in the answers but in the question. As a test for true worship the whole scene was wrong from the start, because the parents were asking the wrong question. If worship is giving something to God, what does "getting something out of the service" have to do with it? Our self-oriented society finds such a question normal and important, but when it comes to worship it is actually sinful and irrelevant.

The right question would be to ask, "Did *God* get anything out of your worship today?" For many people, that would change the whole perspective. Now instead of considering himself to be the rightful recipient of benefits, the worshiper sees himself as one who is responsible to give benefits to another. Of course, whenever God's people do what is right in obedience to God's Word, they receive a "blessing" of some sort. The key point, though, is that getting a blessing is not the purpose of worship. The purpose is to give, not to get. As simple as that sounds, it has proven to be elusive in actual practice.

Churches may actually be contributing to the widespread misapprehension of this concept by referring to the room where worship takes place as the *auditorium*.[6] The implication, of course, is that those attending the service constitute the *audience*. What does an audience do? They generally sit in relative silence while others per-

---

[6]Admittedly, a suitable alternative label is difficult to find. Some churches use the word *sanctuary*, but that conjures up associations with the Old Testament tabernacle or temple with the idea of a holy place where God dwells. In the church age God dwells in the hearts of His people, not in a building made of wood, steel, or stone. Whatever word one chooses, it will probably require periodic explanation to avoid the wrong connotations.

form on stage. When the show is over, they usually express their approval with a nice round of applause. Many churches have actually adopted that practice in recent years, applauding the special music and even the sermon, thus reinforcing the audience concept. It is no surprise, then, that people typically enter a worship service expecting those on the stage (the song leader, choir, soloists, or pastor) to "perform" to their satisfaction. What is revealing is that in this performer/audience mentality, there is no role for God.

The necessary correction requires a new way of thinking about the worship service. First, the people in the pew are not the audience, they are the worshipers. That involves active participation, not passive observation. Those up front on the platform are not performers, they are more like prompters who effectively guide the worshipers through the process. In one sense it would be more appropriate (according to the imagery) if they were behind the curtain while the worshipers pictured themselves as on the stage. Then where is God? He is the "audience" that everyone should be trying to please.[7] His approval means everything, because giving Him glory is the very purpose of worship.

Right Worship Must Conform to the Right Pattern (John 4:23–24)

Everyone seems to have his own ideas about what worship should look like, and most are willing to assume that they are right. That is fine, of course, as long as one is willing to make adjustments when God brings him face to face with the truth. John 4 records a fascinating encounter between Jesus Christ and a woman who was willing to change her thinking. Christ began the conversation with the gospel, because this Samaritan woman was a sinner in need of the Savior (her later testimony to her neighbors indicates

---

[7]John MacArthur, Jr. credits this perspective to Søren Kierkegaard. *The Ultimate Priority* (Chicago: Moody, 1983), 104–5.

that she decided to accept Christ's offer of living water). Once she discerned that the One speaking to her possessed supernatural knowledge, she turned the discussion to the current debate about forms of worship (19–20).[8] Christ answered her question by redirecting her focus: the physical place of worship is not the ultimate issue. At some point in the future neither of the two current options, Mt. Gerizim in Shechem or Mt. Moriah in Jerusalem, would be available (21). In the meantime, however, the Jewish location was right for two reasons. First, contrary to the Samaritans, the Jews based their worship on biblical revelation. Second, God's plan was to provide the Savior through the Jewish lineage (22). In the next two verses Christ addresses the heart of the issue in what is probably the most important passage on worship in the New Testament (John 4:23–24).

> But the hour cometh, and now is, when the true worshippers shall worship the Father in spirit and in truth: for the Father seeketh such to worship him. God is a Spirit: and they that worship him must worship him in spirit and in truth.

The opening statement is puzzling. The coming time is a reference to either the church age[9] or the millennial kingdom when the people of the world will come to Jerusalem to learn how to serve the Lord (Isa. 2:1–3). Everyone will then give the Lord true worship. That does not mean, however, that people should just wait until then. It is time to worship the Lord the right way right now,

---

[8]Actually, this was not a change of topic. Christ was in the process of converting a non-worshiper into a true worshiper of God. It was appropriate for her to connect her need for salvation with the need to know how to worship. John Piper's statement rings true: "Missions is not the ultimate goal of the church. Worship is. Missions exists because worship doesn't." *Let the Nations Be Glad: The Supremacy of God in Missions* (Grand Rapids: Baker, 2003), 11.

[9]D. A. Carson, *The Gospel According to John* (Grand Rapids: Eerdmans, 1991), 224.

which implies, of course, that true worship is possible. It also implies that false worship now is common. The stipulation that true worshipers must follow a certain pattern indicates that worship that fails to do so must necessarily be false. What is this pattern that distinguishes true worship from false? It is worship in spirit and truth. The fact that both *spirit* and *truth* share one preposition in the Greek text (both here and in v. 24)[10] unites the two nouns in some sense, perhaps indicating that each depends on the other and cannot exist in isolation. Whatever *spirit* and *truth* refer to, true worship requires both.

The word *spirit* is evidently a reference to the human spirit of the individual worshiper. His worship must occur with his inner spirit. How else could he do it? He could worship with his body only. That is, Christ is stating that mindless, mechanical worship is not true worship at all. The inward part (the spirit) must participate in the process reflected in the motions of the outward (the body) in order for God to receive glory.

Truth is equally essential. If there was any doubt about what Christ means by this word, His words recorded in John 17:17 clear it up. He prayed: "Sanctify them through thy truth: thy word is truth." To worship in truth, then, means to regulate one's worship according to the instructions of God's Word. In other words, true worship must be scriptural (do it the way God says), and it must be spiritual (do it from your heart).

The last part of verse 23 should serve as a wake-up call for all who desire to please God. The Father is actively, continually seeking people who will worship Him by following the pattern Christ has just described. It is appropriate to infer from this statement that

---

[10]This is not a textual variation (the Majority Text has no second ἐν either). The NIV joins the KJV in adding a second preposition before the word *truth*, but the following translations reflect the Greek text more literally: ESV, NASB, HCSB, and NET Bible.

God is not satisfied with the current quality or quantity of worship He is receiving. He is looking for something more and something better. Apparently worship is often not scriptural, not spiritual, or neither. In one sense the seeker-friendly movement has identified a key concept, except that by striving to please people they have been focused on the wrong seeker. God is the most important seeker, and we should not disappoint Him by turning Him away empty in His pursuit of true worship.

Then Christ ties this biblical pattern of worship directly to the nature of God (24). By His very nature God is spirit.[11] That means that God is not restricted to bodily existence. Rather than being localized to one space, the Father is present everywhere. Wherever someone may be as he engages in the process of worship, then, God is there to evaluate his efforts, determining whether or not his worship is true.

Christ's statement may also include one more aspect: since God is spirit, His evaluation is not limited to the worshiper's body. Not only is He there watching the action, as spirit He also has full access to the spirit of the worshiper. On the other hand, we can evaluate only what we see on the outside. During a worship service it might appear to an observer that everyone is giving God true worship. They stand or sit on cue, participate in the singing, and even have something to give in the offering. Everything looks fine. God goes one step further by actually examining the heart of the worshiper. Even when it looks like true worship to other people, God can see when the condition or attitude of the heart makes

---

[11]Most Greek students learn this principle in their first few years of study: "The presence of the article identifies, and the absence of the article qualifies." As an anarthrous noun, πνεῦμα in this sentence is not indefinite (as reflected in the KJV, which adds the English indefinite article); it is qualitative. God exists with the quality or attribute of spirit. See Carson, *John*, 225.

the worship false. That is why it is necessary[12] for those who worship God to follow the pattern He has described. Worship must be spiritual and scriptural.

THE ELEMENTS OF RIGHT WORSHIP

After my first few years of pastoral ministry, I became concerned about the worship in my church. We were doing everything the way most Bible-believing churches have been doing it for a long time, but that no longer seemed to be a good enough basis. Tradition can be comfortable even when it is not biblical. How did I know that we were not leaving out some essential element of worship, or that we were including an aspect that did not have a biblical basis? As a father I was feeling the responsibility of leading my own family in true worship (Exod. 20:5), but in addition to that, as a pastor I sensed a need to know that I was leading the fathers in my church as they led their own families. I decided to embark on a biblical study of worship.

After I gathered a list of every passage that contributed to the subject of worship, I organized those passages into categories. Some columns on my paper included more verses of Scripture than others, but they seemed to point to five distinct elements that constitute true worship. The results of that study were not startling, but they were life-changing. I realized that one element of worship was missing from our service, and one aspect of our service was not part of biblical worship. Moreover, those things that we were doing that had a biblical basis all required improvement. We needed to be more deliberate and purposeful in our worship. The following elements of true worship represent those five categories on my list, and the verses we will consider are those from each category that I believe state the biblical principles most clearly.

---

[12]The Greek construction has the word δεῖ followed by a present infinitive, indicating a continual necessity.

Preparation Gives God Glory (Eccles. 5:1–3)

The book of Ecclesiastes seems to be an unlikely place to find instruction about worship, but we must leave that matter to the Holy Spirit. Technically this is not so much an actual element of worship as it is an essential prerequisite. At the same time it may well be the most neglected principle of worship. Many people give little or no thought to worship prior to the beginning of the worship service. According to this passage, that could be a serious problem.

> Keep thy foot when thou goest to the house of God, and be more ready to hear, than to give the sacrifice of fools: for they consider not that they do evil. Be not rash with thy mouth, and let not thine heart be hasty to utter any thing before God: for God is in heaven, and thou upon earth: therefore let thy words be few. For a dream cometh through the multitude of business; and a fool's voice is known by multitude of words.

Prepare for Worship Before You Arrive

Verse 1 portrays a person who is traveling to the place of worship. Before he arrives at his destination, however, he must address some important issues. The opening exhortation is not simply a call to guard against stumbling along the path or the possibility of taking a wrong turn. The concern here is that the worshiper may approach the Lord casually, without adequate preparation. Michael Eaton confirms that to guard one's steps "refers to demeanor and preparedness as one comes to worship."[13] Those who regularly enter their public worship opportunities without any preparation might wonder if it really matters. Here are two somber warnings that should cause all would-be worshipers to think again.

---

[13]*Ecclesiastes*, in The Tyndale Old Testament Commentaries, ed. D. J. Wiseman (Downers Grove: InterVarsity, 1983), 97.

The first danger of unprepared worship is that in spite of good intentions the event will turn out to be merely foolish sacrifice. In Scripture the word *fool* refers not to one's intellectual capacity but to his disregard for biblical principles in daily life. God has much to say about practical issues, but the fool supposes that he can get along just fine on his own.[14] That is bad enough when it applies to human relationships, but it is even worse when it affects one's response to God. God provides instructions about how to worship Him, so to ignore His commands is not just foolish, it is rebellious. That becomes even clearer with the warning in the last line of verse 1, which identifies thoughtless worship as nothing less than evil.[15] Ignorance is not a valid excuse, either, because God has revealed what He wants in His Word.

How can one avoid the sin of foolish sacrifice? According to verse 1, the key is to listen to God, which of course includes obeying God.[16] The text does not specify exactly what God might be saying as the worshiper approaches. It is perhaps more likely to refer to something God has already said in His Word about one's attitude toward and preparation for worship. In other words, God expects us to take certain steps before walking into the place of worship.

Psalm 122:1 suggests one possibility that has to do with attitude: "I was glad when they said unto me, Let us go into the house of

---

[14]Derek Kidner identifies כְּסִיל as the most common Hebrew term for "fool" in the book of Proverbs (50 occurrences). See his helpful essay in *The Proverbs*, in The Tyndale Old Testament Commentaries, ed. D. J. Wiseman (Downers Grove: Inter-Varsity, 1964), 40–41. Note that in the Hebrew Bible and in the Septuagint, Eccles. 5:1 occurs as 4:17.

[15]רַע is the moral opposite of what is good and right, and according to *TWOT* depicts "that condition or action which in his (God's) sight is unacceptable." R. Laird Harris, Gleason Archer, Jr., and Bruce K. Waltke, *Theological Wordbook of the Old Testament* (Chicago: Moody, 1980), 2:855.

[16]Eaton (*Ecclesiastes*, 97–98) says it well: "*Listen* refers to heeding as well as hearing."

the Lord." Unfortunately, joy is probably not the most common emotional response when it is time to go to church. In fact, the hectic pace of activity typical of many households as they attempt to depart from their home on time is more conducive to anger and frustration. When people stay up too late the night before, fail to get out of bed early enough, rush about trying to get ready, and arrive for worship irritated and distracted, what does it say about worship? It says that worship is not very important. In order to experience joy when one approaches worship, one must make worship the priority. Too often God's people simply fit worship around their busy schedules. When that schedule has not allowed sufficient time, one's attitude toward worship suffers. On the other hand, if people would deliberately establish worship as their highest priority, fitting the rest of life around this central activity, the prospect for joy in the process would increase dramatically.

Families could no doubt think of numerous ways to make their theology (i.e., worship is important) fit their practice. Here are a few suggestions:

Reorient your thinking to view the Sunday worship service as the highlight of the week.

Plan Saturday evenings to ensure sufficient rest to be fresh and alert for the Lord's Day.

Prepare clothing in advance to eliminate some of the household frenzy on Sunday morning. Anticipate what could go wrong (by experience!), and make appropriate adjustments.

Make successful worship a matter of prayer, acknowledging that you need God's help.

Prepare for Worship After You Arrive

People can do much at home that would help eliminate foolish worship, but personal responsibility does not stop there. Ecclesiastes 5:2 seems to shift the focus slightly. Since the worshiper receives a warning about hasty words "before God," it is likely that he has now arrived at the place of worship and is ready for the service to begin. At least he thinks he is ready. Although the natural tendency may be to start singing a hymn of praise (or whatever element of worship opens the service), something important is missing. Rather than mindlessly rushing into God's presence, pause to prepare your heart for worship through quiet meditation.

Verse 2 suggests that such meditation could flow in two directions. First, think about God (look upward). That He is in heaven is a fitting reminder of His majesty and glory. A few moments of reflection on God's exalted position should serve to focus attention on Him. Up to that moment, the worshiper has been thinking about many other things. It is necessary to recognize that you have now entered the very presence of the God of the universe. That reality should both calm the heart as you eliminate distractions and stir the heart as you anticipate the experience. Scripture does not endorse the current trend toward casual familiarity with God, as if He is one of our buddies. Psalm 99:1–3 (ESV) calls for the appropriate attitude of reverence and awe:

> The Lord reigns; let the peoples tremble!
>
> > He sits enthroned upon the cherubim; let the earth quake!
>
> The Lord is great in Zion;
>
> > he is exalted over all the peoples.
>
> Let them praise your great and awesome name!
>
> > Holy is he!

After meditating on God's position in heaven, think about your position on earth (look inward). The point seems to be that you are just an earthling, unworthy to enter into His presence in your current condition. You need His help. That includes seeking His forgiveness for any sin that would disqualify you from worship. Psalm 24:3 asks an important question: "Who shall ascend into the hill of the Lord? or who shall stand in his holy place?" The answer comes in the next verse: "He that hath clean hands, and a pure heart; who hath not lifted up his soul unto vanity, nor sworn deceitfully." No one fulfills those high requirements naturally. The implicit exhortation calls for confession of sin and forgiveness in order to cleanse both hands and heart.

Hebrews 10:22 provides New Testament confirmation: "Let us draw near with a true heart in full assurance of faith, having our hearts sprinkled from an evil conscience, and our bodies washed with pure water." God invites us into His presence, but we need His grace in order to enter there. Take the time to ask for it.

Ecclesiastes 5:3 may seem to stray from the subject, but it actually contributes an important explanation that lets the reader know that in some ways modern life is not much different from the ancient world. The interpretation hinges on the words *dream* and *business*. In this context of worship, a dream may be more like our day-dream, pointing to someone who is having difficulty concentrating on the worship service. What is distracting him? The business of his life is still occupying his mind.[17] This could include his actual

---

[17]J. Stafford Wright expresses this view well: "The proverb may speak of the false thinking that comes through preoccupation with one's own affairs. When we come before God, our minds are full of our own business rather than with the worship of God." "Ecclesiastes," in *The Expositor's Bible Commentary* (Grand Rapids: Zondervan, 1991), 1168. See also Eaton, *Ecclesiastes*, 99. Some translations explicitly support this interpretation (NIV: "As a dream comes when there are many cares," and NET Bible), some allow it (KJV and ESV), while others seem to go in another direction, which is not very clear (see NASB: "For the dream comes through much effort" and HCSB).

means of employment, but it also could refer to his ambitions for the rest of the day, the conversations and experiences of the morning, and even the sights and sounds around him at that moment. With all these interesting things dominating his attention, he is not thinking about worship. What is the result? The many words that come out of his mouth while he is in that condition (whether saying or singing) are nothing more than the voice of a fool. Lack of preparation deprives God of the worship He deserves.

God's people must take steps to avert the disaster of foolish worship. Arriving a few minutes early is a good start and allows some time to prepare the heart. If the order of service does not begin with a segment devoted to quiet meditation, the worshiper can create that opportunity for himself by taking his seat before the service begins and bowing in prayer. A few verses from the Psalms can provide an appropriate reminder of God's characteristics that deserve worship or a description of what biblical worship requires.[18]

My study of Ecclesiastes 5:1–3 several years ago prompted some changes both in my home and in my church. Besides implementing the suggestions I mentioned earlier with my family, I decided to change how our church opened our worship service. We had always begun with a hymn of praise to the Lord, but I observed that many people were still settling into their places during the first stanza or two. That meant that they were not prepared and that real worship was not taking place at that time. One solution has been to initiate a public call to worship by reading a few verses from the Psalms, then providing a few moments for silent, individual prayer. At that point I lead in a public prayer seeking God's

---

[18]I have accumulated a list with more than 200 passages that serve as a call to worship (enough for a four-year rotation). After reading the verses, I provide a few comments highlighting what the passage teaches about worship. Here are a few random examples: Pss. 4:5; 33:1–3; 48:9–10; 57:11; 99:9; 118:19–20; 145:3–4.

help as we attempt to worship Him during the coming service. After that prayer, we begin with a hymn. My perspective is that worship actually begins when we begin to sing; everything before that is just preparation.[19] Preparation is essential, however, because God has revealed in His Word that He requires it.

Praise Gives God Glory

One summer while I was traveling with my family on vacation, we attended a Sunday morning worship service at a Bible-believing church. The service provided an excellent opportunity for us to give the Lord glory, and the people of that church were a blessing to us in many ways. One thing concerned me, however, that I observed during the congregational singing. The pastor, seated on the platform with his pastoral staff, was engaged in conversation with the man next to him. Later, while the choir was presenting the music they had prepared for that service, the pastor was reading his sermon notes. Then I glanced down at the printed program I had received when we entered and noticed the heading: the words *Preaching Service* appeared in bold letters across the top.

That was when I understood. In that pastor's perspective the service was all about preaching. Everything that occurred before he entered the pulpit was merely "preliminary" to the sermon. The congregational hymns, choir and soloist were not so much ways to worship the Lord as they were means for preparing the hearts of people to hear the message. This is actually a common viewpoint in many churches, and it is not difficult to see why: people need

---

[19]Those few minutes before worship begins also provide an opportunity to take care of other matters that are not directly a part of worship. When I have announcements that require a verbal mention, I prefer to include them before the call to worship (otherwise this was the aspect of our service that I decided to eliminate). These minutes would also be an excellent time to introduce guests or let people greet one another. An alternative, of course, would be to interrupt the worship by taking a short break in the midst of the service to take care of such things.

to hear the faithful exposition of the Scriptures. The supposition that proclaiming the truth of God's Word is the only valid aspect of worship, however, misses the point of God's Word. There are several other elements of worship, and all of them are essential.

Be Careful How You Sing

Perhaps the most obvious way for people to give glory to God is through verbal praise. One could do that individually, of course, by giving a personal testimony of God's goodness or greatness. In order for God's people to praise the Lord together with a unified message and form, however, no vehicle works quite as well as music. The book of Psalms is full of exhortations to praise the Lord with song. Psalm 100 is an excellent example that can serve as the focal point for this discussion:

> Make a joyful noise unto the Lord, all ye lands. Serve the Lord with gladness: come before his presence with singing. Know ye that the Lord he is God: it is he that hath made us, and not we ourselves; we are his people, and the sheep of his pasture. Enter into his gates with thanksgiving, and into his courts with praise: be thankful unto him, and bless his name. For the Lord is good; his mercy is everlasting; and his truth endureth to all generations.

Verse 1 contains several important points that deserve attention. Notice that the opening imperative has wide application: "all the earth" (so ESV and others) must join in the activity. God deserves praise from all His creatures, but particularly those who know the Lord should recognize their duty to participate in congregational singing. Common excuses such as "I don't like to sing" or "I don't have a good voice" are not valid. No essential element of worship is optional. Personal preference or pleasure is not the determining factor. God's Word says to sing, so people should sing. Furthermore, one should assume that the Holy Spirit chose the words of this text deliberately. The call is for a "joyful noise," not necessarily a beautiful sound.[20] Not everyone has the personal ability to produce musical sounds with his voice that are pleasing to others. The reality is that the singing of some people sounds terrible, even when they are doing their best. Their singing might be distracting or even offensive as a solo or in a small ensemble, but as one member of a congregation where everyone else is singing as well, they are welcome to participate. Indeed, God requires them to participate.

Another requirement is that the sound the individual produces must reflect joy. The reiteration in the second line makes it clear that this is an important distinction. As a response to a biblical command, praise is an important duty. Often the one issuing a command is not very concerned about the emotional status of those who serve him. All that really matters is that they obey. God goes beyond mere obedience, however, insisting that His servants adopt a certain manner. Indeed, since this is also a command, it is the duty of God's people to praise Him with joy. This duty, then, must become a delightful task; otherwise it fails to fulfill the purpose.

As simple as it seems, though, joyful praise is actually a great challenge for God's people. Somehow congregations become content with singing songs that honor the Lord without the corresponding manner of delivery. It is surprising to some when they hear that God is not pleased with such singing.

---

[20]The ESV mirrors the KJV in this phrase, but many other versions render the verb as "shout" (NASB, NIV, HCSB, and NET Bible). The parallel exhortation in verse 2 with its specific reference to singing, however, indicates that the sound should be loud, not non-musical.

It reminds me of a newspaper cartoon that portrayed a man behind a huge desk holding the button on the intercom as he talked to his assistant in the next room. The caption read, "Miss Jones, I just realized that today is Secretaries' Day. Send yourself some flowers and a nice note." No one supposes that Miss Jones was very excited about her employer's gesture. Doing the right thing in the wrong manner nullifies the intended honor. Neither should we be surprised that praise offered without genuine joy fails to please the Lord.

Verse 3 identifies the basis for that joy as the greatness of God. He is the God Who made us, and we belong to Him. Such objective truth about Who God is should prompt hymns of praise sung with hearts (and expressions) of joy. The last two verses introduce another element of worship manner: we must sing with thanksgiving. Appropriately, in this case the basis is the goodness of God as seen in His love (*hesed*) and faithfulness (5). This is a more subjective aspect of truth, the response of God's people to their experience as recipients of His grace. The greatness of God produces gladness, and the goodness of God produces gratitude. Both reach expression when God's people gather together to sing praise to the Lord.

The book of Psalms reflects both the objective (Godward) and subjective (manward) orientation of praise. Some psalms focus primarily on God's objective greatness (such as 29, 93, 148), while others focus more on His subjective goodness (such as 9, 23, and 103). The vast majority, however, combine both features. Whereas praise seems to fit more naturally under the objective heading, balanced worship will include hymns that reflect both biblical categories.

Besides numerous calls for congregational response to truth about God, Scripture also includes references to other aspects of musical praise. Psalm 150, for example, lists several different kinds of musical instruments that are appropriate for worship. It is possible that the psalmist intends those instruments to serve as accompaniment to singing, but the text gives no explicit indication of such a limitation. Second Chronicles 5:13–14, on the other hand, describes singers and instrumentalists who were responsible to work together to praise the Lord:

> It came even to pass, as the trumpeters and singers were as one, to make one sound to be heard in praising and thanking the Lord; and when they lifted up their voice with the trumpets and cymbals and instruments of musick, and praised the Lord, saying, For he is good; for his mercy endureth for ever: that then the house was filled with a cloud, even the house of the Lord; so that the priests could not stand to minister by reason of the cloud: for the glory of the Lord had filled the house of God.

In this case both the vocal and instrumental musicians were trained specialists (12). That they accomplished their goal of a unified sound indicates that they had rehearsed ahead of time. Verse 14 makes it clear that the Lord was pleased with their efforts. Scripture, then, endorses the use of skilled musicians who prepare music for the purpose of praising the Lord. The biblical emphasis, however, focuses primarily on congregational singing as the heart of this element of worship.

Be Careful What You Sing

The New Testament also includes important instructions about the use of music in church. Two passages in particular address the use of music to praise the Lord.

> Speaking to yourselves in psalms and hymns and spiritual songs, singing and making melody in your heart to the Lord. (Eph. 5:19)

> Let the word of Christ dwell in you richly in all wisdom; teaching and admonishing one another in psalms and

> hymns and spiritual songs, singing with grace in your
> hearts to the Lord. (Col. 3:16)

In both passages Paul is referring to the public services of the
church where people have the opportunity to sing together.[21] The
actual songs themselves occur in three categories, although their
exact identity is debatable. The first seems to derive from the book
of Psalms, but the others seem to include human compositions
apart from canonical sources. What is clear is that the content of all
three categories reflects the truths of God's Word, with the result
that the participants both convey and receive biblical instruction
and exhortation.[22] The lyrics, then, must undergo careful scrutiny
to ensure that each song is not only doctrinally valid but valuable
as a teaching tool. That is, if a particular song says something true
but is not helpful toward edification, it would not pass the test.
This might eliminate many of the popular "praise choruses" that
sometimes simply repeat trite phrases over and over again. Furthermore, both passages require that the production of musical sound
include the heart as well as the voice. Worship music accomplishes
its purpose only if the heart really believes what the voice is saying.
Because the object is too important for pretense, there is no room
for mindlessly going through the motions of praise.

What is that ultimate purpose? Paul had already hinted at a doxo-
logical focus by his use of the words *psalms* and *hymns*, both of
which describe songs of praise to God.[23] Also, the word *grace* (Col.
3:16) is better translated *thankfulness*, one of the characteristics of

---

[21]The plural Greek reflexive pronoun occurs in both passages, translated *to yourselves*
in Eph. 5:19 and *one another* in Col. 3:16.

[22]Ryken observes, "Like everything else in a worship service, the singing of the congregation (and choir) is a Word-communicating activity." *City on a Hill*, 61.

[23]David P. Nelson notes the dual functions of doxology and edification in worship music. "Voicing God's Praise," in *Authentic Worship*, ed. Herbert W. Bateman IV
(Grand Rapids: Kregel, 2002), 150–54.

true musical praise. Both passages state the explicit goal of music in the church, however, in the emphatic final position: "to the Lord." Thus Paul closes these verses by pointing to God as the object of the music.

Paul's emphasis strikes at the heart of much contemporary worship, where our egocentric culture has infiltrated the church. People want to be entertained, and many churches are willing to accommodate them, performing music that pleases their audience.[24] That focus is unbiblical because true worship is all about God. When the goal is to honor God rather than please man, the musical style of worship will portray a commitment to excellence and beauty that fully supports the rich truths of lyrics chosen for their integrity and biblical accuracy. According to Scripture, this is what God expects.

Prayer Gives God Glory

D. L. Moody once accepted an invitation to preach in a large city auditorium. The building soon filled with people eager to hear the great evangelist. Early in the service Moody asked a pastor from a nearby church to lead in prayer, but about fifteen minutes later the man was still praying. Moody glanced at the crowd and noticed that some were heading toward the exit. Realizing that the long prayer was jeopardizing his opportunity to preach the gospel, Moody stepped to the pulpit and said with a strong voice, "While our brother finishes his prayer, we will join together in a song." Relieved and amused, people returned to their seats.

Most people would probably agree that prayer is not usually the most exciting part of a worship service. In fact, some churches have

---

[24]Ryken (*City on a Hill*, 63–68) has an excellent discussion of this issue, including the pertinent reminder that people of all kinds can be affected by an entertainment mindset: "These warnings apply every bit as much to traditional worship as they do to contemporary worship" (65).

concluded that prayer is not a part of worship at all. Other than a brief prayer at the beginning and perhaps another at the end, the trend is to eliminate prayer from public services. The way prayer usually happens in church services, it is not a very worshipful experience anyway. As in Moody's service, public prayer is often little more than a sleepy interruption to the service. How does that give God glory?

Yet Isaiah 56:7 indicates a direct connection between worship and prayer, calling the place of worship a "house of prayer." Christ confirmed the role of prayer in public worship by quoting this verse as He expelled the merchants from the temple (Matt. 21:13). God's Word indicates that prayer is an essential part of worship and provides insight about how to use prayer to give God glory. A typical worship service may include several prayers: an opening prayer could focus on seeking God's help for the service itself, and a closing prayer could apply the lessons of the worship experience to the week ahead. A prayer before the offering would focus on that aspect of worship. The topic under consideration now, however, is a separate prayer solely for the purpose of worshiping the Lord.

Follow the Pattern
Public prayer is a unique expression of worship. In order for a congregation to sing praise to God with unity and coherency, it is necessary for the people to learn music that someone has written ahead of time. There is no opportunity for spontaneity of expression. Prayer is one aspect of worship that can overcome that limitation. Of course, churches that follow a more liturgical style of worship often forfeit the advantage of spontaneity by reading or reciting pre-written prayers. As elegant and worshipful as such prayers can be, there is no biblical precedent for that practice.[25]

[25]Many of the psalms are, in fact, prayers addressed to God. We lack explicit instances, however, of people actually *praying* those prayers as an act of corporate wor-

The public prayers recorded in the Bible appear to be the product of the moment, expressing the heart of God's people. At the same time, as with other aspects of worship, even prayer is subject to the abuses that can lead to false worship. The elements of false worship (see chapter 3) are no more acceptable for prayer than they are for praise. We should expect God to provide sufficient instructions to help us know how to offer prayer that truly pleases Him and accomplishes His purpose. Although every biblical prayer provides an implicit example, the Lord's Prayer is the only prayer recorded in Scripture that God explicitly identifies as a pattern for His people to follow:

> After this manner therefore pray ye: Our Father which art in heaven, Hallowed be thy name. Thy kingdom come. Thy will be done in earth, as it is in heaven. Give us this day our daily bread. And forgive us our debts, as we forgive our debtors. And lead us not into temptation, but deliver us from evil: For thine is the kingdom, and the power, and the glory, for ever. Amen. (Matt. 6:9–13)

Effective prayer does not need to be long and drawn out. Christ introduced this prayer with a caution (7–8) against needless repetition and mindless babble (ESV: "Do not heap up empty phrases"). Those who do not know God often pray in that way, but it does not accomplish any purpose. In fact, the prayer that Christ presented for His disciples' use is remarkably brief.

A few considerations also indicate that the Lord did not intend for His people to simply repeat this prayer verbatim. First, He said to pray "after this manner" or "like this" (ESV and others), not "with

---

ship. Indeed, the headings that provide musical instructions (e.g., Psalm 4) indicate that their intended use fits the category of praise better than that of prayer. Many of our current hymns also address God directly, but we typically *sing* them rather than *pray* them.

these words." Besides, Luke also records the Lord's Prayer (11:1–4) with wording that is somewhat different. Second, in Luke's account Christ was responding to a request from the disciples. They said, "Lord, teach us to pray," not "Lord, teach us a prayer." Finally, although Scripture records some instances of the disciples praying, there is no evidence that they ever simply repeated this prayer word for word. Repeating the Lord's Prayer in unison is not a violation of any biblical principle, but neither is it the fulfillment of Christ's intended use.

If the Lord presented this prayer as a model for people to follow, then we must analyze its structure to determine what categories He expects us to include in our prayers, whether public or private.[26] The entire prayer divides into two parts, beginning with an expression of devotion to God (Matt. 6:9–10). The first point of concern in prayer is for the worshipers to commit themselves to honor the Lord. For God's name to be "hallowed" is a call for people to treat Him as holy, set apart as special, or sanctified.[27] Whatever else, God must receive glory. (Already the appropriateness of this prayer for a worship service is obvious.)

The next verse identifies another way to express one's devotion to God: commit yourself to obey Him. God's will always finds complete submission in heaven, of course, so that becomes our goal on earth as well. The eschatological fulfillment will occur in the millennial reign of Christ on earth. Until then we continue to pray,

---

[26]Christ may have provided a hint that He intended the principles of this model to apply to public prayer by using the plural form of the verbs in His brief introduction; literally, "When you [plural] are praying, you [plural] be saying" (ὅταν προσεύχησθε λέγετε, Luke 11:2).

[27]The Greek word is ἁγιάζω. *TDNT* suggests that the form represents a divine passive: "The logical subject of sanctifying is God alone and not man." *Theological Dictionary of the New Testament*, ed. G. Kittel, G. W. Bromiley and G. Friedrich (Grand Rapids: Eerdmans, 1964). Ultimately, of course, God is behind the accomplishment of His will, but the prayer would seem to include human submission as well.

acknowledging that for God's people Christ is king already. On the personal level, then, this prayer is actually a request that God's grace would enable the individuals offering the prayer to honor and obey the Lord right now.

The second half of the Lord's Prayer brings us into more familiar territory, although just for a moment. It seems that concern for personal needs often dominates the prayers of God's people. A typical prayer might begin by expressing gratitude for some blessing (too often nothing more than thanking Him for "this day"), but then quickly becomes little more than a shopping list of needs and wants. Such shallow self-focus is not appropriate for private prayer, much less for public worship. The biblical starting point is devotion to God, as we have seen, not benefits from God.

Nevertheless, verse 11 introduces the category of personal needs. If one wonders how this contributes to worship, the answer is that it expresses dependence on God. God receives glory when His people acknowledge that they cannot exist without His help. This statement, then, asks for God's help with physical needs. The request is modest (enough for the current day) and focused (food). At the same time it is representative of all the needs for every day, with the implication that tomorrow the Lord should hear a similar request. God is concerned about all the physical needs of His people, and He encourages them to tell Him what physical challenges they are facing, whether food, shelter, employment, health, or safety. Satisfaction with whatever God provides demonstrates both trust in His care and submission to His will.

Still under the heading of dependence on God, the Lord's Prayer immediately moves on to seek God's help with spiritual needs. Verse 12 is a request for forgiveness for past sins, expressed under the imagery of a debt one owes to God. Since no one can ever pay that debt, the only hope is His forgiveness.

The second phrase of verse 12 sees a link between our sins against God and the sins of others against us. God sets the pattern, promising to forgive us every time we ask. He then expects us to follow that pattern, forgiving others when they ask. Not only does the Lord's Prayer itself acknowledge this link, but Christ reaffirms the connection in the next two verses, both positively and negatively. God is not obligated to forgive those who refuse to forgive others.

Because sin is not just a problem of the past, verse 13 shifts the focus to the need for God's grace when facing the challenges ahead. Past experience is enough to convince us that we are weak when temptation comes our way. "Lead us not into temptation" does not imply, though, that God places temptations in our path. Rather, it acknowledges that temptations are already lurking every day and asks that the Lord would deliver us from them. Victory over evil always depends on God's grace.

Since the Lord provided a model, we must understand the principles of prayer that this pattern portrays in order to follow Christ's example. For the sake of clarity, then, here is a concise structural outline of the Lord's Prayer from Matthew 6:9–13, simple enough for all to follow:

    I.   Express your devotion to God (9–10).
        A.   Commit yourself to honor Him (9).
        B.   Commit yourself to obey Him (10).
    II.   Express your dependence on God (11–13).
        A.   Seek His help for your physical needs (11).
        B.   Seek His help for your spiritual needs (12–13).

As a pattern to follow, the Lord's Prayer provides not only the categories for biblically balanced prayer, but the priorities and proportions as well. God's people should begin where the Lord's Prayer begins, focusing on the Lord before turning to personal requests. Each segment of prayer should also reflect the symmetrical balance of the model prayer. In other words, if one feels inclined to elaborate on the various aspects of his physical needs, he should also strive to elaborate on the other categories to roughly the same degree. A prayer that spends ten seconds expressing devotion to God followed by ten minutes describing personal needs cannot claim to have biblical balance. Sometimes public prayer has a similar lack of balance, such as when intercession for the sick dominates the worship prayer. Pastors, too, should strive to follow the example Christ provides.

Follow the Leader

Public prayer is a key opportunity for pastors or other spiritual leaders to demonstrate before their people how to pray biblically, setting an example that applies to private prayer as well.[28] While the pastor is actually uttering the prayer, however, what should the congregation be doing? There are several options. First, the people could simply listen to the prayer. That seems to be too passive to count as actual worship, although successfully resisting the urge to sleep or daydream can require considerable effort. Second, some worship leaders encourage their people to use the time to pray their own prayer to the Lord. This has the advantage of multiplying the number of prayers that God hears, but it also seems to miss the point of group prayer. Rather than achieve the effect of many prayers that happen to generate from one location, group prayer should be one prayer that generates from many people. That would help portray the sense of unity that corporate worship should maintain.

---

[28]I urge my seminary students to use the personal pronoun that reflects the right mental perspective when they lead others in prayer. If public prayer is simply a personal prayer that happens to occur in public, then the singular pronoun is appropriate ("Lord, *I* praise you for your faithfulness"). On the other hand, if public prayer actually represents the entire congregation as voiced by one person, then the plural pronoun is better ("Lord, *we* praise you"). The distinction may seem small, but it is significant.

The third option, then, is for the each individual in the congregation to follow carefully the one who is leading in prayer and pray his prayer along with him. Matthew 18:19–20 provides the biblical basis for this perspective on public prayer:

> Again I say unto you, That if two of you shall agree on earth as touching any thing that they shall ask, it shall be done for them of my Father which is in heaven. For where two or three are gathered together in my name, there am I in the midst of them.

In this passage Christ clearly commends public prayer, even in its smallest proportions. If at least two or three participate together, He guarantees success. The requirement, though, is that they must "agree" with each other. The Greek word calls for harmony or mutual consent.[29] Failure to fulfill the required condition would forfeit the promised benefit. The only way for everyone to agree is for everyone to pay attention, consciously assenting to the statements that the leader is expressing. In other words, each one must pray the same prayer silently that the leader prays audibly. This requires deliberate, earnest, even strenuous, effort from all. The advantage,[30] however, will be worth it: Christ promises that God will answer that prayer.

Before some get excited about the idea of getting whatever they want, we must note the basic assumption that such prayer will be biblical. The Lord's Prayer has already stipulated that we must submit to God's will and seek His honor above our own. This is not a blank check, then, but an enhanced opportunity to give God

---

[29]The word συμφωνέω is the source for our English word *symphony*. It occurs in Luke 5:36 to describe a patch that does not match the original piece of cloth and thus causes a tear. Those who hear a public prayer must match the one speaking the prayer.

[30]The pronoun αὐτοῖς is a dative of advantage.

glory. Christ assures us that the Father will respond to that kind of prayer.

Verse 20 adds another important factor: Christ attends public prayer. Gathering in Christ's name means under in His authority and to accomplish His purpose. The promise of His presence in the midst of such a group strikes us as odd. Isn't Christ there when only one believer is present? Of course, Christ is not implying that He is interested only in groups, not individuals. When a child of God is all alone, Christ is always there beside him.

This verse, however, goes beyond that. Christ is present with a group of believers gathered in His name in some special way. We struggle to understand in *what* special way, because Christ has not defined it for us. Perhaps we should be content just knowing that group prayer is special, letting that be sufficient motivation for us to utilize public prayer. An analogy, though, might help.

If a citizen appears before the governor petitioning for a certain cause, the governor may listen and choose to respond. If that petition has the signature of 100 other citizens, and they are all standing outside his office door, he might be even more likely to respond. If, however, his own son was standing in the group, lending his assent to the worthiness of the cause, the hope for response would increase dramatically. Perhaps that portrays the value of public prayer: not only many people petitioning God together, but God's Son standing among them.

On mission trips to Poland and other Eastern European countries, I have often enjoyed the privilege of participating in the times of prayer that usually conclude their worship services. Several individuals take the opportunity to lead in prayer, each in turn, while everyone stands in front of his seat. One feature makes it obvious that they understand the process and value of public prayer. When each one finishes his prayer, all the others respond with a hearty "Amen!" They shout the word with such conviction that it is almost startling to the foreigner listening in. Perhaps what is most startling is that they actually take their responsibility in public prayer seriously. I have often thought at such times, "What a great example for us!" What a difference it would make if we could learn to participate in public prayer like that. Why does that matter? Because the Lord would receive much more glory from our worship service if we would follow these instructions in His Word.

Presentation Gives God Glory

Some pastors and theologians are not sure that giving in the offering is an aspect of worship at all.[31] According to the motivational words that often introduce this segment of the service, the primary reason for the offering is to help the church meet its financial obligations. As such, it seems to be more of an interruption to worship than an act of worship. God's Word, however, does not support that perspective, providing sufficient evidence to conclude that giving to God is an essential element of worship. In fact, the offering constitutes another significant advance beyond the other acts of worship.

As noted previously, praise by its very nature is a distinctly unified expression of worship, but it lacks spontaneity. Prayer adds an important degree of spontaneity, but since only one person can lead in prayer at one time, it lacks individuality of expression. That is where giving in the offering contributes its own unique opportunity. Each individual worshiper has the freedom to express his personal devotion to God according to his own means and desire.

---

[31]Barrett, for example, in a chapter entitled "The Liturgy of Worship," lists what he calls "the biblically mandated elements of worship" (*The Beauty of Holiness*, 78) as reading Scripture, praying, preaching, and singing, but he does not mention giving in the offering. Ryken, on the other hand, does (*City on a Hill*, 61).

From this perspective giving in the offering provides balance to the overall worship experience. It remains, however, to demonstrate that this is the biblical perspective.

Present Your Tithe to God

Whether or not God requires the tithe during the New Testament era is an open issue of debate among God's people. Some see the tithe as a stipulation of the Mosaic law that does not apply to the church. They reason that God specified particular items and amounts that He expected the people of Israel to give to Him, but in the church age we have liberty to give whatever amount we choose. This seems to correspond to the distinct advantages we enjoy over previous dispensations, such as the completed canon of Scripture and the indwelling of the Holy Spirit. The argument seems to be that God now entrusts His people with the responsibility to discern for themselves how much they should give Him.

On the other hand, this seems to discount too greatly the role of the Old Testament in the lives of God's people today. A paucity of references to a certain topic in the New Testament does not necessarily indicate that God is no longer concerned about that issue or that He has changed His expectations. It is at least possible that God believes the Old Testament revelation on a given subject to be sufficient, with no need to reaffirm or elaborate in the New Testament. Any study of worship in the Bible, for example, will face the reality that the vast majority of information comes from the Old Testament. Does that mean that worship is not as important in the church as it was for Israel? Hardly anyone would think so. A better conclusion is that the Old Testament laid such a good foundation on the subject that there was little more for the New Testament to reveal. That might be a valid perspective concerning the offering as well.

Of course, the forms of worship have changed from the Old Testament to the New. In order to learn the Old Testament lessons, it is necessary to observe the worship forms, discern the principles behind them, and then apply those truths to modern circumstances and opportunities. For example, worship for the nation of Israel centered largely on the tabernacle and temple, complete with adorned priests, elaborate rituals, and various sacrifices. None of those features is available today, but they teach much about what pleases God and gives Him glory. Indeed, during the early days of the church, believers continued to worship at the temple as long as they were welcome there (Acts 2:46; 3:1). Paul continued to participate in some of the Old Testament worship forms well into the church age (Acts 21:26). When the temple was no longer available, it is likely that the church continued to apply these Old Testament principles of worship, incorporating them into their church worship services in new ways.

The situation with giving in the offering is similar. Consider Deuteronomy 12:5–6:

> But unto the place which the Lord your God shall choose out of all your tribes to put his name there, even unto his habitation shall ye seek, and thither thou shalt come: and thither ye shall bring your burnt offerings, and your sacrifices, and your tithes, and heave offerings of your hand, and your vows, and your freewill offerings, and the firstlings of your herds and of your flocks.

Although many of the Old Testament forms of giving are no longer available or appropriate, the principles are still valid. The principle in verse 5, then, is that God expects His people to assemble for worship at the place He designates, even though the location has changed. Many of the specific items an Israelite could give to God do not apply to us, partly because animal sacrifice is not part of church worship and partly because we do not live in a primarily agricultural society (those who don't own sheep or farmland cannot give a firstborn lamb or first fruits to God). Such inherent restrictions would eliminate five of the seven items listed in verse 6. The two remaining items, the tithe and freewill offerings, are no less available or appropriate in our day than in the Old Testament era. In this case we have the opportunity to fulfill the biblical principle by using the same biblical form. It is entirely possible, and I believe even likely, that tithes and offerings continue to be part of God's expectation in the church age.[32] We will consider these one at a time.

To begin with, it is important to note that the tithe was not the exclusive property of the Mosaic law. The Old Testament indicates that the practice of giving the tithe existed about four hundred years before Moses. As Abraham returned from the battle over Chedorlaomer and the Mesopotamian kings, he gave ten percent of the spoils of war to God's representative, Melchizedek (Gen. 14:18–20). Furthermore, when Jacob realized the extent of the blessings God was promising him, he responded by committing himself to worshiping the Lord, including giving ten percent of God's provision back to Him (Gen. 28:20–22). We do not know how the patriarchs first discerned that a tithe would please God, since we have no record of revelation on this point during their era. By including this specific number in the Genesis record, however, Scripture seems to confirm that the amount was at least appropriate, if not expected, even before the Mosaic era.

The Mosaic era, of course, included the tithe among its numerous requirements. Toward the end of that era, Jesus Christ took one

---

[32]It is interesting that only the tithe is subject to question. Few seem to doubt that freewill offerings are both appropriate and even necessary.

opportunity to commend the tithe even while rebuking the Pharisees for their selective disobedience to God's law:

> But woe unto you, Pharisees! for ye tithe mint and rue and all manner of herbs, and pass over judgment and the love of God: these ought ye to have done, and not to leave the other undone. (Luke 11:42)

The Pharisees' zeal for giving God the tithe He required was admirable, extending all the way to counting the leaves as they harvested their garden herbs. At the same time, their disdain for doing what God required regarding justice and devotion was abominable. Christ's message included two main points: tithing does not replace godliness, but neither does godliness replace tithing. At least at that point in salvation history, God still required both.

The rest of the New Testament is silent on this matter. Rather than point to the absence of a verse that confirms the tithe during the church era, perhaps we should notice the absence of a verse that withdraws it from the category of God's expectations. Since no such verse exists, I suggest that the tithe continues unchanged since the earliest biblical examples of worship, although it is not the only form of monetary giving that ought to characterize worship.

Present Your Offering to God

While the tithe can demonstrate one's submission to God as an act of obedience to His command, the freewill offering can indicate the degree of one's devotion to God. Paul highlights this feature when he urges the Corinthians to participate in the offering: "I speak not by commandment, but . . . to prove the sincerity of your love" (2 Cor. 8:8). By its very nature, a freewill offering is unspecified as to amount: "Every man according as he purposeth in his heart, so let him give; not grudgingly, or of necessity: for God loveth a cheerful giver" (2 Cor. 9:7). If the amount is a personal decision, does that mean that participation in the offering is optional? Not according to Psalm 96:7–8. As part of the call to give God glory, this passage specifically commands the worshiper to "bring an offering, and come into his courts" (8*b*). How much to give He does not say; just bring something to give. Deuteronomy 16:16–17 presents a similar command, expressed even more strongly (the key phrase is identified by italics):

> Three times in a year shall all thy males appear before the Lord thy God in the place which he shall choose; in the feast of unleavened bread, and in the feast of weeks, and in the feast of tabernacles: and *they shall not appear before the Lord empty*: every man shall give as he is able, according to the blessing of the Lord thy God which he hath given thee.

The expected frequency of public worship was different, by necessity, for the nation of Israel from what it is now. What might typically be a ten- or fifteen-minute drive for us might have involved a five-day walk for them (each way). Due to the distance and other considerations, God required Jewish men to assemble at the place of worship only three times each year. The frequency of worship is a matter of Old Testament form, but verse 16 concludes with a statement that seems to present an enduring principle: do not approach the Lord in worship without an offering in your hand. Whereas Psalm 96:8 is in the form of a positive command, this verse expresses the same requirement as a negative prohibition. Together both passages suggest that whenever an Old Testament believer worshiped God, God expected him to come equipped with something to put in the offering. Verse 17 goes on to emphasize that the amount is a personal decision based on an assessment of God's provision.[33] Participation in the offering as an act of wor-

---

[33]Verse 17 also seems to confirm that this passage is a timeless statement of principle: it fits as well in Paul's discussion of the offering in 2 Cor. 8–9 as it does here.

ship, however, would seem to be no more optional than singing praise to God or listening to His Word. Unless one can demonstrate that God has changed His mind about this aspect of worship (or can suggest a different interpretation of these verses), it is difficult to avoid the conclusion that without an offering, worship is incomplete.

The Old Testament combines the concepts of tithes and offerings one last time in Malachi 3:8–12. So certainly does God regard the tithes and offerings as His rightful possession that He can charge with robbery those who refuse to give. Furthermore, God declares that His people experience the pain of His curse because they have withheld from Him. If one has any degree of doubt about the application of the tithe during the church age or the necessity to give an offering at every worship service, it would certainly seem wise to err on the safe side.

My personal advice to those who enquire about the dynamics of giving in our age is to suggest a distinction between how to give a tithe and how to give an offering. The individual can determine for himself the frequency of the tithe, but the amount does not change. No matter how often one gives his tithe, if he calculates the amount based on his income since the previous tithe, the resulting total will be the same. For example, if someone receives a paycheck once per month, he could give his tithe once per month, or he could subdivide his tithe and give one portion each week. The freewill offering is just the opposite: the individual can determine for himself the amount of the offering, but the frequency does not change.

Each individual, of course, will need to settle this matter between himself and the Lord. My personal conviction is that God requires an offering every time I assemble with God's people for public worship. That does not necessarily mean, however, every time I meet with God's people. Individual churches are free to define their various services as they see fit. In my perspective our Sunday morning service is when we gather specifically to worship God, striving to include all the essential aspects of worship. Our Sunday evening service often appears to be similar, but our stated purpose for that service is broader, allowing more flexibility. Our Wednesday evening service focuses on prayer. Of course, prayer is an aspect of worship, but it also has application beyond worship. Our Sunday morning service, then, is when we assemble specifically for worship, and I urge our people to come to that service with some offering to present to God.[34]

Preaching Gives God Glory

Many churches are moving away from the direct preaching of God's Word during the worship service. The prevailing trend is to replace the pulpit with a stool and have the pastor offer an informal "talk" or "chat" instead of a sermon.[35] In some cases drama

---

[34]Some have wondered about the propriety of using a collection box at the entrance instead of passing offering plates. On the surface, this seems to follow the biblical pattern more precisely. Mark 12:41 portrays Christ sitting near the "offering box" (ESV) watching people give to God as they walked by. Temple worship, however, was not a group "sit-down" event with a defined beginning and end. From the time an individual entered the temple precincts, he was worshiping. He could participate in the various worship forms at his own pace and leave whenever he was finished. An offering box, then, would be one of the places where worship took place continually. In our day placing a box at the door might tend to separate giving from worship (either before or after the worship service). For that reason I prefer to include the offering during the service, providing the opportunity to present gifts to God as an act of worship. It is also why I use the word *presentation* to label this element of worship.

[35]The seeker-friendly movement has concluded that people do not appreciate preaching. Church marketers have therefore devised means to adapt their product to meet the demands of consumers. John MacArthur, Jr. presents several excerpts of actual newspaper advertisements in which churches tout their new style: "There is no fire and brimstone here. No Bible-thumping. Just practical, witty messages." "Services [here] have an informal feeling. You won't hear people threatened with hell or referred to as sinners. The goal is to make them feel welcome, not drive them away." "The sermons are relevant, upbeat, and best of all, short. You won't hear a lot of preaching about sin and damnation and hell fire. Preaching here doesn't sound like *preaching*. It is sophisticated, urbane, and friendly talk. It breaks all the stereotypes." "As with all clergymen

has become the preferred means to convey the "message" instead of using a monologue format. Apparently, some question not only whether preaching is a necessary part of worship but also whether it has a legitimate role at all.

Is it possible that the traditional order of service has for years allowed a non-worship element to dominate its worship service? That is actually an important question. As I was accumulating the biblical data on worship in my original study years ago, I became concerned about the preaching category. There were plenty of verses describing praise, prayer and giving as elements of worship, but I was not finding many passages that portrayed preaching as an act of worship. Of course, the Bible has much to say about the importance of preaching God's Word, but where was the biblical evidence that establishes a direct, essential connection between preaching and worship? Furthermore, if such a connection exists, what is it about the sermon that gives God glory? Scripture provides the answer to all these questions, with two passages in particular identifying preaching as a necessary aspect of worship.

Worshipers Must Hear God's Word (1 Timothy 4:13)

The apostle Paul expected an opportunity to return to Timothy in Ephesus, at which time he would provide further instruction and assistance in the ministry. In the meantime, however, some issues could not wait and required written reinforcement. Clarity about the central role of God's Word in Timothy's ministry was one such matter of urgency: "Until I come, devote yourself to the public reading of Scripture, to exhortation, to teaching" (1 Tim. 4:13, ESV).

[this pastor's] answer is God—but he slips Him in at the end, and even then doesn't get heavy. No ranting, no raving. No fire, no brimstone. He doesn't even use the H-word. Call it Light Gospel. It has the same salvation as the Old Time Religion, but with a third less guilt." *Ashamed of the Gospel: When the Church Becomes Like the World* (Wheaton, IL: Crossway, 1993), 47.

Paul's primary focus in this verse is the threefold role of Scripture in the public worship service of the church.[36] The first element is the simple reading of God's Word aloud. This was especially important during the early centuries of the church, when personal copies of the Bible were scarce and the primary exposure to God's Word came through public reading. Even when people can read the Bible on their own, however, the public reading of Scripture continues to be an essential element of worship. God has spoken through His written Word, and it gives Him glory when people listen to what He has to say. Thus Timothy (and all who lead in worship) must focus "attention" (NASB) on reading God's Word during the worship service. This would call for an accurate, purposeful reading. When the one doing the reading hurries through the text, making careless errors in wording or pronunciation, he inadvertently communicates the message that this part of the service is not very important. On the other hand, when the reading is careful and expressive, the focus falls on what the text actually says, providing a better opportunity for the living Word to penetrate deep into the hearts of the listeners.

The next two aspects of the ministry of God's Word in 1 Timothy 4:13 actually comprise a single event in the worship service that logically follows the reading. This is Paul's summary of the sermon—exhortation and teaching—and both parts are essential. Before examining what they are and how they work, we should first consider why they are important.

---

[36]George W. Knight III argues for the public nature of all three elements, concluding, "Thus Paul urges a public ministry that reads the scriptures to the gathered Christians, exhorts them to respond appropriately, and teaches them its principles." *The Pastoral Epistles*, in The New International Greek Testament Commentary (Grand Rapids: Eerdmans, 1992), 207–8.

According to 2 Timothy 3:16–17, God "breathed out" His Word (ESV) for a specific purpose: to make people "perfect" (KJV).[37] The clear implication is that apart from God's Word people are imperfect or incomplete. Bryan Chapell calls this the "Fallen Condition Focus."[38] It is our "fallen condition" because of the effects of sin, and it is a condition that every person shares to varying degrees (depending on one's individual progress in sanctification). In order to correct what is wrong in the lives of people and supply what is missing, God provided His written, inspired Word. In other words, God designed every portion of Scripture to correct and change specific aspects of people's fallen nature. It is the preacher's responsibility to discern, through careful exegetical text analysis, the target the Holy Spirit had in mind when He wrote any particular passage of Scripture. Once he has isolated the Fallen Condition Focus of the text, he is ready to prepare and then preach a sermon that provides the distinct message of the text that every listener needs.

This brings us back to the last two components of 1 Timothy 4:13. Every sermon, according to Paul, must include both teaching (truth: what people must know) and exhortation (application: what people must do) derived from the text of Scripture. This is not only a biblical command to preachers, it is also the precedent set by preachers in the Bible. For example, Mark 1:15 summarizes the entire preaching ministry of Jesus Christ in two parts: Christ preached both truth—"The time is fulfilled, and the kingdom of God is at hand"—and exhortation—"Repent ye, and believe the

---

[37] The Greek word beginning verse 17 (ἵνα) introduces a purpose clause and means "in order that." The word translated *perfect* is a Greek adjective meaning "complete, capable, proficient." Frederick Danker, ed., *A Greek-English Lexicon of the New Testament and Other Early Literature*, 3rd ed. (Chicago: University of Chicago Press, 2000), 136.

[38] *Christ-Centered Preaching: Redeeming the Expository Sermon*, 2nd ed. (Grand Rapids: Baker, 2005), 48–55. This excellent book is essential reading for every preacher of God's Word.

gospel." In Acts 2:40, Luke summarizes Peter's Pentecost sermon the same way: "And with many other words did he testify [truth] and exhort [application]." Every preacher, then, should be able to summarize his own sermon in a two-part statement of truth and exhortation that reflects the message of the text.[39] He is then ready to expound that text, explaining the truth the listener needs to know and applying that truth to everyday life.

Worshipers Must Respond to God's Word (Psalm 95:6–8)

One more question remains: how is the sermon a component of worship? Does the simple act of preaching and/or listening to God's Word sufficiently give glory to God, or does God expect something more? Psalm 95:6–8 provides the answer:

> O come, let us worship and bow down: let us kneel before the Lord our maker. For he is our God; and we are the people of his pasture, and the sheep of his hand. To day if ye will hear his voice, Harden not your heart.

This is clearly a psalm about worship, providing in these verses both the appropriate action ("bow down") and the biblical basis ("He is our God"). The sentence that bridges verses 7 and 8, however, is where we find the specific connection between worship and the Word of God. That sentence begins with a conditional clause, which introduces a degree of uncertainty. In a worship service people certainly ought to hear God's voice through the preaching of His Word. Two factors, however, explain why there might be some doubt.

First, there may be a problem with the preaching. Perhaps the worship service did not include the preaching of God's Word. That

---

[39]Chapell calls this summary the *proposition*, which is the direct answer to the FCF: "A formal proposition is the wedding of a universal truth based on a text with an application based on the universal truth" (144).

would be a serious deficiency. Even if there was a line in the order of service labeled *sermon*, it is possible that the preacher was declaring his own thoughts rather than expounding what God says. A pastor may have some good things to say, and they might correspond with the truth of God's Word. He might even use one or more texts from Scripture to show that God agrees with him, but if he has not expounded the Word of God, it is possible that his listeners will not hear what God has to say. [40] Expositional preaching based on careful exegesis of the text is the only way to guarantee that people will have the opportunity to hear God's voice.[41] Preachers bear an enormous responsibility that requires a daily dependence on God as they strive to discern the message of the text and then deliver that message clearly to their people. If they fail, those people cannot truly worship God.

If the preacher succeeds in his task (by God's grace), there is still a second obstacle that might prevent the message from getting through: the people might not be listening. Hearing God's voice

---

[40]Bill Hybels believes that preaching must interest unbelievers. His sermons typically have focused on "their marriages, their priorities, their emotions, their finances, their parenting, their quest for fulfillment, their sexuality." Bill and Lynne Hybels, *Rediscovering Church* (Grand Rapids: Zondervan, 1995), 174. But later in his book he offers a startling admission that contradicts his own practice: "Watch out for going overboard with 'felt-need' or 'helpful' messages. When you're involved in a seeker ministry, it's tempting to go for long periods of time on what I call junk-food preaching diets. In other words, giving people biblical wisdom to improve their relationships, smooth their emotions, deal with their daily problems, and put some zip back in their marriage. . . . The reality is that you'll never grow up fully devoted followers of Christ on a diet of spiritual Twinkies" (185).

[41]MacArthur issues a powerful call for expository preaching: "For those of you who want to preach the Word accurately and powerfully because you understand the liability of doing anything less; for those of you who want to face the judge on the day of reckoning and experience the Lord's pleasure with your effort; for those of you who are eager to let God speak His Word through you as directly, confrontively, and powerfully as He gave it; and for those of you who want to see people transformed radically and living godly lives, there is only expository preaching." John MacArthur, Jr., "Introduction," in *Rediscovering Expository Preaching*, ed. Richard L. Mayhue (Dallas: Word, 1992), xvii.

is not just a matter of transmitting sound through air waves. Successful listening includes hearing the sound and letting the message reach the heart. No preacher can accomplish that on his own: the hearer must be *listening.*

Effective communication requires two active components, one generating the message and one receiving the message. If the listener fails to cooperate, whether through active refusal or passive lack of interest, He has not heard God's voice. Too many listeners are ready to blame the preacher for their failure to comprehend, but the reality is that they may be responsible as well. Someone intent on worshiping the Lord must do his part to hear God's voice while the preacher presents the sermon.

Even if both the preacher and the listener have fulfilled their respective communication responsibilities in a particular worship service, so that the condition in verse 7 has been met, there is still one more crucial step before actual worship has taken place. Hearing God's voice is just the condition that opens the opportunity to worship God. Verse 8 exhorts the action that brings the whole process to its towering climax: "Harden not your heart!"

God speaks for one reason only: to change the lives of people. No matter what text the preacher expounds, God wrote that text to change something that is wrong or provide something that is missing in the life of every listener (2 Tim. 3:16–17). The only possible response that gives God glory is confession (admit that God is right in His assessment of your condition) and repentance (seek His forgiveness and the grace that can bring conformity to His standard). Anything less than that indicates a hardened heart. The person who fails to respond has not worshiped God.

This is why it is so important for the preacher to identify both the Fallen Condition Focus and the proposition from the text. The

Fallen Condition Focus reveals to the listener his current needy condition before God. The proposition summarizes God's answer to that problem as expressed in the passage of Scripture. Jesus Christ is the crucial link between where the listener is and where he ought to be. That is, only Christ can bring a sinner to salvation or move a saint along the path toward Christlikeness.[42] No matter what the need and no matter what the text, the preacher points the listener to Christ as the only hope for victory (Col. 1:27–28). Because worship requires every listener to respond to God's Word, the preacher closes the message by urging each person to turn to Christ for forgiveness and grace.[43] When the listener does that, he has given God the glory He deserves.

---

[42] This is the key to "Christ-centered" preaching. See Chapell's presentation in chapters 10 and 11.

[43] The expectation that every person must respond to God's Word every time makes a general altar call somewhat impractical. Instead, I have adopted the practice of providing a few moments of silence after the message to allow each person to respond to God individually, assuming most need no help to do so. Then I invite those who are unsure how to respond (especially those who do not know Christ) to come during the closing hymn for counsel and prayer.

2

MULTI-GENERATIONAL IMPACT: WORSHIP STYLE AND YOUR FAMILY

It is popular in our day for churches to offer variety in worship. Church signs listing the schedule of services often indicate that they offer a traditional worship style at one service and a contemporary style at another. A third alternative is the "blended" service, in which both styles occur together, supposedly satisfying both sides. The clear implication is that worship style is simply a matter of personal preference. The individual worshiper is free to choose which style he likes best, while the church is obligated to provide whatever people want.

This has become particularly important in the market-driven church movement, where churches often determine the format of their worship service based on community surveys.[1] That is, not only are churches giving attendees a choice of style, but even unsaved people have a say in how churches conduct their worship. A huge assumption lies behind all this variety: that worship style does not matter to God. The thinking seems to be that as long as

---

[1] Bill Hybels was an early leader in this approach, and his Willow Creek Community Church continues to influence thousands of church ministries around the world. Hybels and his wife, Lynne, have recorded their ideas and experiences in *Rediscovering Church*. G. A. Pritchard conducted an intensive examination of Willow Creek's methodology over the course of 2½ years and published his findings and critique in *Willow Creek Seeker Services: Evaluating a New Way of Doing Church* (Grand Rapids: Baker, 1996). Recently Willow Creek has been re-evaluating its strategy after a research study indicated that many of their most committed members were not satisfied with the church's contribution to their spiritual growth. The results of that study were published in Greg L. Hawkins and Cally Parkinson, *Reveal: Where Are You?* (Barrington, IL: Willow Creek Association, 2007).

people are pleased, God is satisfied with any kind of worship. Since many churches that have adopted this philosophy have grown to mega-size, it seems to make sense to many people. Do we know, however, that God agrees? Is it possible that He is not as excited about people-oriented worship as people are? Are sincerity of heart and the personal enjoyment of the worshiper the only important considerations? Is there an objective standard of right and wrong in worship style? Of course, the only way to know what God thinks about this issue is to examine His Word.

GOD PUNISHES WRONG WORSHIP

The book of Genesis portrays various people engaged in the act of worship (e.g., Noah and the Patriarchs) and occasionally records God's response (e.g., Cain and Abel), but the first biblical legislation about worship comes in Exodus 20.

God Declares His Disdain for Wrong Worship

The first two of the Ten Commandments relate directly to worship, providing important insight on God's perspective. There are a few interpretive challenges, however, that demand attention before one can understand what God is saying about worship. First, both commandments seem to be prohibiting essentially the same action.

> Commandment 1: "Thou shalt have no other gods before me." (Exod. 20:3)
>
> Commandment 2: "Thou shalt not make unto thee any graven image, or any likeness of any thing that is in heaven above, or that is in the earth beneath, or that is in the water under the earth: thou shalt not bow down thyself to them, nor serve them." (4–5a)

Is there a difference between these two commands? A closer look reveals that there is an important distinction and that the sequence of the two commands is crucial to the message they convey. The first prohibits the worship of all false gods. The assumption is that the reader intends to comply with this first command and focus all his worship on the only true God. That is, the worshiper has now removed all false gods from consideration and is ready for the next instruction from God.

Then the second commandment advances the thought by prohibiting the use of images in worship even when people design them to represent the one true God.[2] To summarize, the first commandment prohibits giving true worship to false gods, while the second prohibits giving false worship to the true God. The key principle here for our study is that God has particular ideas about how people should and should not worship Him. In other words, it is not enough to worship the right God; the Lord also demands that people worship Him in the right way. Moreover, He claims the prerogative to determine what constitutes right worship.

Therefore, there is a right and wrong in worship style. Next, we would want to know how important this issue is to God. Is this just a slight preference for certain kinds of worship, with a willingness to tolerate and even appreciate other forms, or is God's concept of acceptable worship strict and exclusive? This brings us to the second interpretive challenge, in Exodus 20:5. The rest of this verse presents a disturbing portrait of God and His revealed response to violations of the second commandment.

> First corollary to commandment 2: "For I the Lord thy God am a jealous God, visiting the iniquity of the fathers upon the children unto the third and fourth generation of them that hate me." (5*b*)

---

[2]For details see John I. Durham, *Exodus*, in Word Biblical Commentary (Waco: Word, 1987), 285.

This statement has provoked much discussion and concern. It seems to indicate that God punishes children when their fathers fail to give Him the kind of worship He demands. The problem, of course, is that this seems to be inherently unfair to the children. Theologians and commentators have provided some suggestions that attempt to explain and present this principle in a more acceptable manner. Before considering these interpretations, however, it is important to recognize that this is not an obscure statement buried in some dark corner of the Old Testament. After all, this is one of the Ten Commandments. Furthermore, Scripture repeats this principle, in whole or in part, five more times, extending into the period of the Babylonian exile.[3] Such distribution and repetition demand an honest reckoning with the truth that this statement asserts, whatever that truth might be.

One common method of alleviating the sense of unfairness is to view God's involvement as a more indirect role. That is, when a father indulges in sin, his children often suffer as a result. Those effects, however, are in the category of natural consequences rather than direct acts of punishment from the hand of God.[4]

It is true, of course, that in God's providence one person's sin often affects the lives of other people, sometimes to a dramatic degree.

---

[3]The other passages are Exod. 34:7, Num. 14:18, Deut. 5:9–10 (the 2nd reading of the Ten Commandments), Deut. 7:9, and Jer. 32:18. Some have supposed that the rejection of the "sour grapes" proverb in Jer. 31:29–30 and Ezek. 18:2–3 indicates that by the sixth century BC God was no longer punishing children for their fathers' sin. The presence of the punishment principle in Jer. 32, however, demonstrates that there is no inherent contradiction between this principle and the concept of individual responsibility and that God was still incorporating both in His dealings with people at that time.

[4]An all-too-common example in modern society is the tragic effect that drunk driving often has on innocent people. Such events, however, are not restricted to instances when a father drives while intoxicated, nor are the consequences limited to his own family members. R. Alan Cole suggests the following examples: "slavery, exploitation, imperialism, pollution, immorality." *Exodus*, in The Tyndale Old Testament Commentaries, ed. D. J. Wiseman (Downers Grove: InterVarsity Press, 1973), 156.

The question here, though, is whether or not that is the point of Exodus 20:5. The word *visiting* seems to support the concept of natural consequences with its possible implication of indirectness. The Hebrew word *paqad*, on the other hand, although it has a broad range of meaning, conveys a very direct activity: God investigates a situation carefully and responds with the appropriate action.[5] The generic sense of the word is evident in that the response can be either positive or negative, depending on the result of the inspection. This case is clearly negative (God discerns iniquity), so it is appropriate to translate *paqad* as *punish* in this verse.[6] This eliminates the likelihood of an indirect role for God. Furthermore, the next verse has a parallel statement about the positive effects on children when fathers choose to obey God. Since the Lord is actively involved in the distribution of blessings in verse 6, He must also be actively involved in the application of punishment in verse 5. Besides, the sin in this context is wrong worship. What would be the natural consequences of wrong worship?

Ultimately, the natural consequences view does not alleviate the sense of injustice anyway. If it is unjust for God to punish children directly for the sins of their fathers, it would also be unjust for Him to allow them to suffer misery, pain, poverty, or even death because of their fathers' sin. God is just as responsible for providence as He is for punishment.

---

[5]The *Theological Wordbook of the Old Testament* (Chicago: Moody, 1980), 2:731 provides a helpful description of פָּקַד: "The basic meaning is to exercise oversight over a subordinate, either in the form of inspecting or of taking action to cause a considerable change in the circumstances of the subordinate, either for the better or for the worse."

[6]When פָּקַד occurs in negative contexts in which it means *punish*, the Hebrew word עַל usually precedes the object of the punishment. In Exod. 20:5 the word עַל occurs three times, preceding the words for *children, third,* and *fourth.* See Francis Brown, S. R. Driver, and Charles A. Briggs, eds., *A Hebrew and English Lexicon of the Old Testament* (Oxford: Oxford University Press, 1907), 823.

Another popular interpretation assumes that God includes the children in the punishment only when the children actually participate in committing the sins of their fathers. The phrase "them that hate me," then, would include both the fathers and their children. This view effectively eliminates the problem of injustice. Unfortunately, it also practically eliminates the meaning of the passage.

It is true, of course, that God punishes people for their own sin. If that is what Exodus 20:5 means, then including the father-child relationship in the statement of this equation would be a roundabout way of saying it. Even worse, it would be a false way of saying it. Does God here state His intention to punish only three or four generations of sinful people, letting all later generations of sinners go free? Such a ridiculous suggestion exposes the inherent weakness of this viewpoint. Besides, careful exegesis reveals that the text itself will not support this interpretation. The phrase "them that hate me" translates a Hebrew participle with a prepositional prefix. The preposition expresses a genitive relationship, which the English translations reflect with the word *of*, meaning "belong to" them that hate me.[7] Thus the text attributes the sin to the fathers alone, not the children.

What does it mean to "hate" God? The word *hate* does not necessarily imply that one detests or loathes an object. In fact, it may represent a relationship in which someone simply neglects one person because he prefers another.[8] In this context it describes

---

[7]This is the genitive by circumlocution. See E. Kautzsch, ed., *Gesenius' Hebrew Grammar*, trans. A. E. Cowley (2nd ed.; Oxford: Oxford University Press, 1910), sec. 129 a and e, and S. R. Driver, *The Book of Exodus* (Cambridge: Cambridge University Press, 1929), 195.

[8]The same Hebrew word also occurs in Gen. 29:31, expressing that Jacob hated Leah. The previous verse, however, makes it clear that Jacob did not despise Leah: "he loved . . . Rachel more than Leah" (Gen. 29:30).

someone who does not love God enough to give Him the kind of worship He desires. Thus God concludes that someone hates Him when that person chooses to disregard the second commandment. The converse occurs in the next verse: those who love God obey the second commandment. This agrees with Christ's perspective when He said, "If ye love me, keep my commandments" (John 14:15).

God Demonstrates His Disdain for Wrong Worship

The exegetical evidence, then, indicates that this passage means what it seems to say. When fathers worship the true God in the wrong way, He punishes their children.[9] The attempts to interpret the statement otherwise miss the mark. Is there any biblical evidence, though, that God has actually acted on this principle? In fact, there are several possible historical instances,[10] but one stands out as particularly appropriate for this study.

---

[9]Deut. 24:16 seems to contradict this conclusion: "The fathers shall not be put to death for the children, neither shall the children be put to death for the fathers: every man shall be put to death for his own sin." Conservative theologians who defend the integrity and unity of the book of Deuteronomy recognize that the author would not contradict in chapter 24 what he has already asserted in chapters 5 and 7. (Even redaction critics should question whether an editor would allow such a blatant error.) Several textual issues indicate that this passage is not a direct reference to the Exod. 20:5 principle at all: the vocabulary is different, there is no mention of the third and fourth generation, and the scope is wider (forbidding punishment of fathers for the sins of their children as well). The context provides the best solution to this apparent discrepancy: this passage describes human administration of justice, not divine punishment. See Anthony Phillips, *Ancient Israel's Criminal Law* (Oxford: Basil Blackwell, 1970), 34; and A. D. H. Mayes, *Deuteronomy* (London: Oliphants, 1979), 326.

[10]Clear instances include the death of the Egyptian firstborn (Exod. 11–12), the death of Achan's family (Josh. 7), and the death of Saul's descendants at the hands of the Gibeonites (2 Sam. 21). In each case the fathers committed the sin without any implication that the children participated. Furthermore, God directed the punishment, condoned it, or carried it out personally. There are also numerous passages that pronounce future punishment on descendants because of their fathers' sin. Some examples include Noah's curse on Canaan (Gen. 9), Jacob's prophecy about Simeon and Levi (Gen. 49), God's declaration about Eli's descendants (1 Sam. 3), the prophecy against Jeroboam's family (1 Kings 14), and Elisha's condemnation of Gehazi (2 Kings 5).

During Israel's wilderness wanderings some became critical of the limitations God had imposed on the public worship rituals (Num. 16). In particular, 250 Levites and a few Reubenites envied the leadership privileges of Moses and the Aaronic priesthood. In verse 25 the story focuses on Dathan and Abiram. Because they refused to appear before the tent of meeting, Moses confronted them at their own tents. At God's direction Moses advised the assembly to evacuate the vicinity near Dathan and Abiram. As their neighbors scrambled to safety, Dathan and Abiram emerged from their tents. Verse 27 specifies that the rebels stood with "their wives, and their sons, and their little children."

The presence of the latter group is important. Whatever the spiritual disposition of the wives and sons (the text does not indicate), the little children were too young to have participated in their fathers' sin.[11] Of course, God had the option of ordering someone to rescue the children, or He could have avoided mentioning their presence in the text (relieving reader anxiety). Instead God not only left the children with their families, He told us they were there, apparently wanting us to note their presence. This dramatic scene then reached its climax as the ground opened beneath them "and swallowed them up" (32). God had punished the children for the sin of their fathers. That sin, as in Exodus 20:5, was a direct violation of God's standards for worship.

One question remains: why would God do that? The answer seems to have something to do with motivation. Most would agree, in theology if not in practice, that worshiping God is man's most important function and reason for existence. There is not general agreement, however, about the importance of worship style, with

---

[11]According to L. Elliott-Binns, the Hebrew word translated *little children* refers to "young children a stage beyond our 'toddlers.'" *The Book of Numbers* (London: Methuen, 1927), 114.

many assuming that how they worship God does not matter. Worship according to personal preference continues to grow in popularity among God's people in spite of written revelation to the contrary, including the second commandment.

Perhaps that is why God attached the corollary. The human desire to design worship that pleases people is so strong that simply telling people not to worship Him the wrong way is not enough. Therefore, God added a motivating statement. When people refuse (or just neglect) to worship God the right way, He chooses to punish their children. What is the connection? To the most important duty (worship) God has attached the most compelling motivation (children). When a person thinks that the consequences for a sinful action will be limited to him alone, he may decide that the momentary pleasure is worth the penalty. When he realizes that God may punish his children for his waywardness, he may think again.

This may help explain why God limits the effect to just the third or fourth generation. Taking the father as the first generation, the punishment can extend as far as his grandchildren and great grandchildren. Why stop there? Because that is as many descendants as most people could expect to see during their lifetime. When a father is deciding what he is going to do, God wants him to be thinking about real family members that he knows and loves. Knowing that God punishes wrong worship in this way should make it harder for people to ignore God's command.

The motivational factor may also shed some light on the punishment principle in Jeremiah and Ezekiel. It is difficult to reconcile the acknowledgment that this principle was still part of God's response to sin at that time (Jer. 32:18) with Jeremiah's (and Ezekiel's) rejection of the "sour grapes" proverb.[12] If God punishes children for the sins of their fathers, why was it inappropriate for the people of that time to use the sour grapes proverb to explain their predicament? After all, the fathers had sinned grievously against the Lord, resulting in great oppression for their descendants living in the homeland (including Jeremiah), while many others endured the hardships of exile in Babylon (including Ezekiel).

The answer lies in the fact that Jeremiah's and Ezekiel's hearers were using the sour grapes proverb to complain about their circumstances. It was a way of saying, "We are experiencing great punishment, but it is not our fault. Our ancestors rebelled against God, but we are innocent." That represented a monstrous abuse of the punishment principle as revealed in Exodus 20:5 (and elsewhere). Children who experience God's punishment due to their fathers' sin might be innocent of that particular sin, but no person is free from sin in general. No one can ever justly respond to any punishment by claiming he does not deserve it. In fact, anyone who is not currently enduring the flames of hell is not experiencing what his sin deserves. God has graciously delayed your punishment (or accepted the payment of Christ's death at your request).

God's rejection of the sour grapes proverb was really a rejection of these people's false claim to innocence. God was using the principle of punishing children for the sins of their fathers, but He was also actively applying the principle of individual retribution, and the latter was more than enough to explain their present circum-

---

[12]More precisely, Jeremiah (31:29) was predicting the demise of the sour grapes proverb during the future golden age (the millennium). Perhaps at that time obedience to God will be so widespread that people will no longer complain about God's methods of punishing sin (or perhaps God will have more limited need to enforce this principle). Ezekiel, on the other hand, seems to call for the immediate rejection of the sour grapes proverb.

stances. The former principle is not a valid excuse for children; it is a motivating device addressed to fathers.

GOD BLESSES RIGHT WORSHIP

For those who might still be struggling with the sense of fairness, the next verse in Exodus 20 might help. God's response to worship is not limited to negative instances.

God Pronounces His Blessing

Exodus 20:6 introduces the possibility that some will choose to render acceptable worship to God and describes what they can expect. As a parallel statement to the last part of verse 5, this verse continues to express the result of God's jealousy, only now in the positive sense: He is zealous to bless those who fulfill their part in the covenant relationship.

> Second corollary to commandment 2: "And shewing mercy unto thousands of them that love me, and keep my commandments."

The Lord describes the nature of His response to right worship with a fascinating Hebrew word. The complexity of *hesed* is evident from the range of English renderings in the various versions: "mercy" (KJV), "steadfast love" (ESV), "lovingkindness" (NASB), "love" (NIV), "faith" (NEB), "covenant faithfulness" (NET), and "faithful love" (HCSB). The key to understanding the concept behind this word is the relationship that exists between the subject and object. Based on that relationship the subject acts with a sense of loving loyalty toward the object.[13] In this passage God promises to remain loyal in love to those who give Him true worship. This is

---

[13]For further analysis of the nuances of חֶסֶד, see Nelson Glueck, *Hesed in the Bible*, trans. Alfred Gottschalk (Cincinnati: The Hebrew Union College Press, 1967); and R. Laird Harris, *TWOT*, 1:305–7.

a powerful statement of lasting commitment, showing the importance of right worship from God's perspective.

The next word identifies the recipients of God's love. The KJV's simple "thousands" reflects the Hebrew, which does not specify a thousand *what*. Most other versions insert the word *generations*, probably based on the parallel in verse 5 (which the words *third* and *fourth* imply). Actually, the KJV could imply multiple thousands and perhaps suggest to some that the beneficiaries include people who sustain a relationship with the worshiper other than that of direct descendants. That this is highly unlikely is clear not only from verse 5, but also from Deuteronomy 7:9. Of the six Old Testament passages expressing the principle that God deals with children based on the actions of their fathers, this is the only one in which the Hebrew word for *generation* actually occurs.[14] This is enough, however, to conclude that all the passages refer to a thousand generations of actual descendants. It is not clear whether this refers to a specific numerical limit (1000 and no more) or a more generally indefinite number.[15] Either way, God guarantees that the benefits of right worship for one's family will go on and on for a very long time.

Exodus 20:6 concludes by specifying the reason for God's blessing on these descendants: their fathers chose to love God. In contrast to the negative statement in verse 5, which offered no explicit explanation for what it means to hate God, this verse has a parallel statement revealing that loving God means to keep His commandments. The plural (*commandments*) indicates that this principle can apply more broadly to other aspects of obedience besides just wor-

---

[14]In keeping with the generally positive perspective of Deut. 7, this passage includes only the positive side of the effects of the fathers' actions on their children.

[15]If a generation is estimated at twenty years, then a thousand generations would be longer than the earth has existed, if the biblical chronogenealogies are taken seriously.

ship. On the other hand, God attached this corollary directly to the second commandment, making worship the primary application. God will bless the family of a man who commits himself to obey God's Word in general, but He particularly wants people to know that He places an especially high priority on worship. To qualify for this blessing, one's worship must be right.

God Demonstrates His Blessing

As with the negative aspect, we might wonder if there are any historical instances of children benefiting from a father's decision to worship God the way He says. Of the positive biblical portrayals, perhaps the best example comes from the life of Abraham.

Scripture introduces Abraham as a man with great potential to be a blessing to others. Of the blessings the Lord offered to Abraham in Genesis 12:1–3, two in particular indicate that others would share in the benefits: "thou shalt be a blessing" (2) and "in thee shall all families of the earth be blessed" (3). In the succeeding chapters God narrowed the emphasis to blessings on Abraham's own descendants.

In order to obtain these and other blessings, Abraham needed to commit himself to obey the Lord. The rest of the Genesis account of his life records Abraham's faithfulness to that commitment (although with some faltering along the way).[16] Genesis 26:5 provides God's summary of Abraham's faithfulness: "Abraham obeyed my voice, and kept my charge, my commandments, my statutes, and my laws." This seems to correspond with the broader application of Exodus 20:6 (with its plural *commandments*) to all God's ex-

---

[16]Robert B. Chisholm, Jr. demonstrates that this arrangement between the Lord and Abraham, known as the Abrahamic Covenant, began as a conditional promise (God would bless if Abraham would obey) and ended as an unconditional oath (since Abraham had obeyed, God committed Himself to provide the blessings). "Evidence from Genesis" in *The Coming Millennial Kingdom: A Case for Premillennial Interpretation*, ed. Donald K. Campbell and Jeffrey L. Townsend (Grand Rapids: Kregel, 1997), 35–54.

pectations of obedience. The final culmination of the Abrahamic Covenant in Genesis 22, however, corresponds to the specific application of worship.

Genesis 22 opens with God proposing a test to discern the depth of Abraham's love for God and commitment to obey His commands. Verse 2 records the sobering details of that test:

> And he said, Take now thy son, thine only son Isaac, whom thou lovest, and get thee into the land of Moriah; and offer him there for a burnt offering upon one of the mountains which I will tell thee of.

This was to be a test of worship. The Lord deliberately designed an act of worship that would not only bring Abraham no pleasure but would be utterly abhorrent.[17] Even the wording of the command seems intent on highlighting the aspects that would make it very difficult for Abraham to obey (Isaac's status as his only son, and the fact that Abraham loves him). There is biting irony here as compared with Exodus 20:6. In this case, choosing to worship the Lord the way He said would seem very bad for Abraham's family, to the point of eliminating all hope that Abraham would ever have any descendants at all.

The pressure on Abraham was enormous: preserve his son or worship the Lord. It must have been a long night for Abraham, although the text gives no hint that he struggled to make his choice, portraying him as rising early the next morning for the journey to Moriah. Finally, at the crucial moment when Abraham was about to complete the worship God had commanded, the Angel

---

[17]The narrator graciously informs the reader from the start that this was only a test, implying that God did not intend to accept a human sacrifice. Of course, Abraham did not know it was a test, and even the reader senses relief when God actually stops the slaughter in verses 11–12.

of the Lord stopped the process and announced that Abraham had passed the test. Verses 16–18 describe God's dramatic response:

> By myself have I sworn, saith the Lord, for because thou hast done this thing, and hast not withheld thy son, thine only son: That in blessing I will bless thee, and in multiplying I will multiply thy seed as the stars of the heaven, and as the sand which is upon the sea shore; and thy seed shall possess the gate of his enemies; and in thy seed shall all the nations of the earth be blessed; because thou hast obeyed my voice.

Notice the emphatic connection between Abraham's obedience and God's response. Because Abraham obeyed God's command to worship the way God said, God committed Himself to blessing Abraham's descendants.[18] Every aspect of this pronouncement is special, but the last clause of verse 17 is particularly pertinent for our study. In the ancient world the city gate was more than just the point of access: it was the seat of city government.[19] To control the gate of one's enemies, then, meant to rule over them. God's promise to Abraham, however, goes one step further: his descendants will actually *possess* the enemies' gate, indicating a permanent position of authority and control. Premillennialists recognize this as nothing less than the millennial rule of Christ, Abraham's seed,

---

[18]This is the final ratification of the Abrahamic Covenant, when the conditional promises became an unconditional oath. From this point God is obligated to fulfill all His promises to Abraham.

[19]This becomes clear in Ruth 4, when Boaz goes to the city gate to transact the redemption of Naomi's property before the elders assembled there. Excavations and restoration of the Old Testament city of Dan in northern Israel confirm this arrangement. Just inside the city gate is a broad courtyard with seating around the perimeter for the elders. In one corner a small stone platform marks the place where the king or city governor would sit on his throne to render decisions. Those unable to travel to the Holy Land to see this site personally can view Todd Bolen's excellent photos of this and other biblical sites. His extensive collection is in the *Pictorial Library of Bible Lands*, a CD series available through his website, http://www.bibleplaces.com.

over all the nations of the world, with the Jewish city of Jerusalem as His capital.[20] Of course, by definition the millennial kingdom will last for only 1000 years. Scripture indicates, however, that God will then transform that temporary kingdom into the eternal reign of Christ on earth, including ethnic Jews, the descendants of Abraham.[21] In other words, God has guaranteed Jewish participation in both the millennial kingdom and the eternal kingdom of Jesus Christ. Why would He do that? Because they have a father who decided to obey God and worship Him the way He said.

FACING REALITY

The punishment of children for the sins of their fathers is admittedly a difficult principle to accept. The clarity of the biblical passages in which it occurs, however, also makes it difficult to deny. Is it possible, though, that God discontinued His use of this principle of punishment with the close of the Old Testament era and the beginning of the church? After all, the occurrences of both the statements of the principle and the historical examples are all limited to the Old Testament. That is unlikely, for two reasons. First, when the Lord first introduced this principle in Exodus 20:5, He connected it directly to His own nature as a God Who is jealous

---

[20]Some theologians point to the reign of Solomon as the fulfillment of God's promises to Abraham. Although Solomon's territory was extensive, the duration of his dynasty was much too short to satisfy God's commitment. Furthermore, long after Solomon was dead, Israel's prophets continued to look forward to a future fulfillment of the Abrahamic Covenant. See especially Mic. 7:20 as well as the testimony of the post-exilic author of 1 Chron. 16:15–18. For descriptions of Christ's kingdom, see Isa. 2:2–4; 9:6–7; 11:6–10; 65:17–25; Jer. 23:3–5; 31:31–37; 33:14–17; Ezek. 36:24–28; Dan. 2:34–35, 44; 7:13–14; Mic. 4:1–4; Luke 1:32–33; and Rev. 20:1–7. The apostle Paul maintains that the covenants still belong to Israel (Rom. 9:4) and in Rom. 11:25–32 looks ahead to the salvation of Israel, quoting OT passages that include the possession of the land in their contexts (Isa. 27:1–13; 59:20–60:22; and Jer. 31:23–40).

[21]See 1 Cor. 15:22–28. Rev. 21 portrays the eternal state as taking place on the new earth with New Jerusalem descending from heaven. John notes that the gates of the city are inscribed with the names of the twelve tribes of Israel, a clear indication of the presence of Jews there. (Of course, that the twelve foundations are marked with the names of the apostles points to the presence of the church as well.)

for the worship that He deserves. The doctrine of the immutability of God maintains that aspects of His character do not change with the passing ages. As long as people are prone to sin, we should expect Him to continue to use the most effective means to encourage right worship. Second, the Bible nowhere announces or even hints that this principle is only temporary. As with other aspects of worship, the best assumption is that the principles that were true in the Old Testament era continue to be true today.

At the same time, God's people must keep this principle in biblical perspective. The punishment of children for the sins of their fathers is not a matter of settled fate, as if once the sin is committed there is nothing you can do to stop the punishment. As with other aspects of sin and other methods of punishment, God offers forgiveness to those who repent. In fact, the second statement of this punishment principle, in a moving self-declaration of God's character, emphasizes God's eagerness to forgive:

> And he passed in front of Moses, proclaiming, The Lord, the Lord, the compassionate and gracious God, slow to anger, abounding in love and faithfulness, maintaining love to thousands, and forgiving wickedness, rebellion and sin. Yet he does not leave the guilty unpunished; he punishes the children and their children for the sin of the fathers to the third and fourth generation. (Exod. 34:6–7 NIV)

Just as sin is a choice, forgiveness is a choice as well. When a sinner turns with repentance toward the God of compassion and love, he will find that God's forgiveness is full and free. The one who refuses to repent, however, will bear his guilt and see the punishment fall on his family.

It is also possible, though, that the family members could plead for God's mercy and ask that God divert the punishment heading their way. There is some precedent for this in a few of the prayers recorded in Scripture. Nehemiah, for example, confessed the sin of the fathers that resulted in the exile and destruction of Jerusalem, asking God to allow him to return to Jerusalem and rebuild the walls (Neh. 1:5–11). Daniel also confessed the sins of the nation of Israel, even though he had not personally participated in those sins (Dan. 9:4–19). Scripture seems to indicate, then, that a person may confess the sins of a father or grandfather with the full expectation that the Lord will hear and forgive.

When the positive and negative aspects of this principle are seen side by side, the fairness issue takes on a new perspective. The liability for sin is great, but it is limited to just the third or fourth generation. The potential for blessing, however, is virtually unlimited (a thousand generations). The Lord has given fathers a great opportunity. Furthermore, if God punished children for the sins of their fathers without telling us that He follows such a procedure, He might be unfair. He has not been secretive, however. On the contrary, He has revealed this truth clearly and repeatedly. If there is still a degree of unfairness, it is not on God's part. He has given fathers a choice. They can give God wrong worship, and God will punish their children, or they can worship God the way He wants, and God will bless their children. When a father continues to ignore God's standards of worship in spite of the revealed consequences for his family, it is that father who is being unfair.

The first time I preached on this principle was to a group of men gathered for a monthly fellowship. I was the guest speaker that Friday evening and chose Exodus 20:4–6 as the text. The fellowship was so encouraging that I decided to join them the following month as well, this time just as an attendee. Early in the evening the host pastor invited men to give a personal word of testimony about how God was working in their lives. One man stood and reflected on the message he had heard at the previous meeting. I was thrilled to hear him say, "God used His Word to change my thinking last month. I walked away from that meeting saying, 'Lord, I never want to sin again.'" That is exactly the kind of response the Lord wants to see. We might give it a little tighter focus: "Lord, by your grace I never want to worship you the wrong way again."

3

THE DANGERS OF DEVIANT WORSHIP

Since the penalty for wrong worship is so severe, the ability to identify wrong worship should be a great concern. Perhaps aspects of wrong worship have crept into our current worship routine. How can we know? Again, the only way to know for sure what worship practices God considers to be wrong is to examine His Word. Scripture presents a number of instances in which God's response to various kinds of worship makes it clear that He regarded that particular worship style as false and unacceptable. The New Testament asserts that the Old Testament records of the experiences of the people of Israel provide intentional lessons for God's people today: "Now these things happened to them as an example, but they were written down for our instruction, on whom the end of the ages has come" (1 Cor. 10:11, ESV). By discerning the timeless principles behind each historical instance, one can better discern which current worship practices might actually be instances of wrong worship.[1]

WORSHIPING THE RIGHT GOD THE WRONG WAY

The worship styles that fall into this category tend to look like blatant, perhaps even deliberate, instances of disobedience, but they

---

[1] John MacArthur suggests four categories of unacceptable worship: (1) "the worship of false gods," (2) "the worship of the true God in a wrong form," (3) "the worship of the true God in a self-styled manner," and (4) "the worship of the true God in the right way, with a wrong attitude." (*The Ultimate Priority*, 7–12). This is a helpful arrangement, but our study does not include category 1, and I have decided to combine categories 2 and 3 because of their considerable overlap.

serve as effective reminders that even God's people can become forgetful of God's Word and deceived into thinking that the Lord is tolerant of deviation.

Worship Based on Imagination (Exodus 32:4–6)

Shortly after arriving at Sinai, Moses ascended the mountain to receive the tablets inscribed with the Ten Commandments, plans for the construction of the tabernacle, and other civil and ceremonial instructions. As the time of Moses' absence extended toward forty days, the people became impatient with the delay and anxious to establish some type of worship. Their words to Aaron express both their request for a worship service and their excuse for not waiting for instructions from Moses: "Up, make us gods, which shall go before us; for as for this Moses, the man that brought us up out of the land of Egypt, we wot not what is become of him" (Exod. 32:1).

This incident does not seem to belong under the heading of "Worshiping the Right God" since it appears that the people of Israel wanted to abandon the Lord and substitute false gods in His place. Several pieces of evidence, however, indicate that they intended to keep the Lord as the sole object of their worship. First, the Hebrew word for *God* in the Old Testament regularly occurs in the plural. Whenever it refers to the one true God, translators render the word as a singular. In this case most translations interpret this passage as referring to false gods and so use the plural.[2] When Aaron complied with their request, however, he produced just one golden calf, to which the people responded with the declaration, "These be thy gods, O Israel" (4). Since they were looking at only one

---

[2]Keil and Delitzsch identify this occurrence as the typical plural of majesty, making this young bull "an image of Jehovah." C. F. Keil and F. Delitzsch, *Commentary on the Old Testament*, trans. James Martin (Grand Rapids: Eerdmans, rpt. 1975), 2:222.

graven image, it is unlikely that they intended their statement as a true plural, either in verse 4 or in verse 1.[3]

Second, the people continued their statement in verse 4 by identifying the golden calf with these words: "which brought thee up out of the land of Egypt." That is a clear reference to a recent historical experience that was still vivid in their memories. Even during the times in Israel's later history when they succumbed to the temptation to worship false gods, there is no indication that they ever forgot which God delivered them from Egypt. Whatever was wrong with their worship on this occasion, this statement shows that they thought they were still worshiping the same God.[4]

Finally, Aaron had a significant response to the people's excitement about the golden calf. He built an altar in front of the calf and then declared, "Tomorrow is a feast to the Lord" (5). The word *Lord* printed in all uppercase letters is the English translators' method of identifying for the reader that the Hebrew text has the proper name for God, often transliterated as *Yahweh* (or sometimes as *Jehovah*). This should be enough to settle the issue: they were choosing the wrong way, but they thought they were still worshiping the true God.[5]

Why did they choose a golden *calf*? From our perspective this does not seem very flattering. We must not suppose, however, that

---

[3]Even though the Hebrew also has a plural verb and pronoun, two translations have decided that the singular sense is more likely (both, however, put the plural in a marginal note). See the NASB and HCSB.

[4]The HCSB seems to be sensitive to this point by capitalizing the word *God* in verse 4, even though it uses lowercase in verse 1 (the marginal note for verse 4 offers two alternate renderings: singular lowercase and plural lowercase).

[5]Durham (*Exodus*, 422) surveys the evidence and concludes: "In demanding such an image, the people have violated, first of all, the second commandment." Also, MacArthur places this incident in his second category, not the first: "When the Israelites constructed the molten calf, they were worshiping the true God, but they had reduced Him to an image" (9).

this statue represented a newly born animal tottering on wobbly legs. The word translated *calf* points to a fully developed ox in the prime of life.[6] This was the most powerful domesticated animal they knew, one that would be extremely useful in an agricultural economy. From their perspective this reflected a very high view of God. On the negative side, though, it also reflected their wrong thinking about God. When they did not need an ox they would simply leave him in the stall or in the pasture. As long as they provided food and water, the ox would be ready to help whenever they called. An ox seemed to be a good way to portray their view of what they thought were God's best qualities.

This is exactly the point: they had devised a form of worship based on their own view of God. Forms of worship that come from the minds of people always reflect the view of God they have in their minds.[7] The problem is that no one has a high enough view of God. Perfect understanding of Who God is would result in perfect trust in His will and perfect obedience to His Word. Until we attain to the glorified state, our conception of God will continue to be deficient. That is why we must not trust humanly conceived worship styles. Only worship forms that God has endorsed in His Word are safe.

Human conceptions of God have not changed much over the centuries. People still imagine that God is a convenient resource

---

[6]R. Alan Cole argues that the word *calf* is misleading: "A young bull in his first strength is meant: for instance, the word can describe a three-year-old animal (Gen. 15:9)." *Exodus*, in The Tyndale Old Testament Commentaries, ed. D. J. Wiseman (Downers Grove: InterVarsity, 1973), 214.

[7]Durham's summary is insightful: "The composite of Exod 32:1–6 is not an account of the abandonment of Yahweh for other gods; it is an account of the transfer of the center of authority of faith in Yahweh from Moses and the laws and symbols he has announced to a golden calf without laws and without any symbols beyond itself. Moses is the representative of a God invisible in mystery. The calf is to be the representative of that same God, Whose invisibility and mystery [sic] is compromised by an image he has forbidden" (421–22).

Whose primary reason for existence is to meet their needs and help make them happy. Furthermore, they think that as long as they give Him His due (once a week should be enough), He will be content to stay out of their way until called upon. Like the ox, He might not always like the way His people treat Him, but He is usually tolerant. The golden-calf mentality is still prevalent today.[8]

What does God think about golden-calf forms of worship that reflect human imagination of what He is like? He describes those who practice such worship as "corrupted" and "stiffnecked" people worthy of immediate destruction (7–10). At Sinai Moses held back destruction through his intercession, but then he provided a graphic demonstration of the sinfulness of their worship by shattering the stone tablets at the foot of the mountain. Next he communicated the bitterness of wrong worship by grinding the golden calf to powder, sprinkling it over the water, and making the people drink it. There can be no doubt: God rejects worship that derives from human imagination rather than divine revelation.

Worship Focused on Innovation (Leviticus 10:1–3)

After much anticipation, Moses erected the tabernacle and prepared its furnishings for use. God's instructions had been meticulously precise down to the last detail. In measurement and material, everything was now exactly the way God wanted it. Even the incense had to be just right, with equal parts of stacte, onycha, galbanum and frankincense (Exod. 30:34). This particular formula was exclusive: not only must they never use this incense for any other purpose (37–38), they must never use any other kind of incense for worship (9). God's Word was clear. Furthermore, the Lord had demonstrated His satisfaction with their complete

---

[8]Philip Graham Ryken suggests that it is even worse in our day because the relativism of post-Christian culture has taught people to develop their own version of truth. As Ryken says, "People now believe in defining their own deity" (*City on a Hill*, 56).

obedience to His worship stipulations by letting His glory appear to all the people and by sending fire from His presence to consume the burnt offering. Judging from the reaction of the people, who "shouted, and fell on their faces" (Lev. 9:23–24), it was an impressive, moving experience.

Apparently Nadab and Abihu, Aaron's two oldest sons, thought they could do even better. They had heard all God's instructions and were newly ordained to lead God's people in worship. The biblical account of what happened next is stark and concise (10:1–2):

> And Nadab and Abihu, the sons of Aaron, took either of them his censer, and put fire therein, and put incense thereon, and offered strange fire before the Lord, which he commanded them not. And there went out fire from the Lord, and devoured them, and they died before the Lord.

Contrary to God's explicit command, they devised their own combination of ingredients to produce a different kind of incense.[9] What were they thinking? Any suggestion would necessarily be speculative, but perhaps they were trying to duplicate the experience God had caused by His display of glory and fire recorded in chapter 9. Alternatively, perhaps they were actually trying to improve on what God had designed. It is entirely possible that Nadab and Abihu had been experimenting with incense and had come up with a product that smelled better than the one God had commanded. On the other hand, maybe they were the first pyrotechnic artists, making the flames sparkle with beautiful colors. Well, maybe not. Whatever was different about their incense, though, the point is just that: it was *different*.

---

[9]It is also possible that Nadab and Abihu obtained burning coals from some source other than the altar (which God had recently lit), but these and other possible aspects of violation of God's prescribed worship procedures are not mutually exclusive. See R. K. Harrison, *Leviticus*, in The Tyndale Old Testament Commentaries, ed. D. J. Wiseman (Downers Grove: InterVarsity, 1980), 109–10.

What does God think about worship that is different from what He commands? Apparently He does not like it at all. Nadab and Abihu were not just reprimanded; they were eliminated, and in dramatic fashion. There is a bit of irony in the sequence here: God's fire, man's fire, God's fire. The One Who has the last word is the same One Who gave the first word. If anyone neglects the first (God's command), he will not miss the last (God's judgment).

Aaron was stunned, but Moses provided an explanation based on something they both already knew, at least theoretically (3): "Then Moses said unto Aaron, This is it that the Lord spake, saying, I will be sanctified in them that come nigh me, and before all the people I will be glorified. And Aaron held his peace." This is an important statement expressing God's purpose for worship. The right interpretation might become clearer by a reading of God's statement with emphasis on the word *I* in both clauses. Those who worship God, and particularly those who lead others in worship, must commit themselves to one purpose only: they must treat God as holy, striving to make sure that He alone receives glory. It doesn't even matter that the motives of Nadab and Abihu might have been good, desiring to make worship more exciting and beautiful so that God would receive more glory. In fact, the danger with innovative worship forms is that they might work! In that case, God would need to share the glory with those who designed the service. Only when God is the designer of worship can worship accomplish its purpose.

We might have expected God to be a little more lenient. After all, Israel had only four priests to begin with. Now there were only two. At the end of the day, though, Aaron had nothing to say. There was no excuse for what his sons had done. God had been clear when He gave His commands about worship, and now He had been clear when assessing human innovation in worship.[10] We will have nothing to say, either, if we pursue worship apart from God's Word.

The parallel with the current church-marketing movement is frightening. When the goal is to attract people through worship styles, those styles must necessarily be innovative. The pressure to provide worship that is fresh, exciting and entertaining is enormous, and next week must be even better. Moreover, who is really getting the glory? The credits identify the writers, the producers, the musicians, the stage crew, etc. What a great show. God, however, is neither impressed nor pleased.

Worship Like the World (Deuteronomy 12:29–32)

As the nation of Israel camped on the plains of Moab just across the Jordan River overlooking the Promised Land, Moses delivered his final messages of instruction and exhortation in the book of Deuteronomy. Moses had much to say about worship, including how to avoid wrong worship. For most of the past forty years God's people had been alone in the wilderness, isolated from the neighboring nations. That was about to change dramatically. In the coming months and years, as they moved from city to city destroying the Canaanites, God's people would be surrounded by pagan culture. Much of that culture involved religious practices, and some of those practices might be attractive and interesting. Should Israel observe the rituals of pagan worship, discern the elements that are acceptable, and incorporate them into their worship of God? Moses provides God's mind on this matter (Deut. 12:29–32):

---

[10]John E. Hartley suggests that by His immediate action against the priests, God was protecting the people: if He had allowed Nadab and Abihu to continue, they would have misled the people, resulting in punishment for all. *Leviticus*, in Word Biblical Commentary (Dallas: Word, 1992), 134.

When the Lord thy God shall cut off the nations from before thee, whither thou goest to possess them, and thou succeedest them, and dwellest in their land; take heed to thyself that thou be not snared by following them, after that they be destroyed from before thee; and that thou enquire not after their gods, saying, How did these nations serve their gods? even so will I do likewise. Thou shalt not do so unto the Lord thy God: for every abomination to the Lord, which he hateth, have they done unto their gods; for even their sons and their daughters they have burnt in the fire to their gods. What thing soever I command you, observe to do it: thou shalt not add thereto, nor diminish from it.

As with the golden calf incident at Sinai, this passage does not address the possibility of forsaking the Lord to worship false gods (although that also became a distinct temptation for Israel). The issue here is adopting the pagan patterns of Canaanite worship for the purpose of worshiping the Lord.[11] Moses refers to this danger as a snare that God's people must guard against (30), indicating that there is a real potential for deception. That is, pagan worship includes some features that may be appealing to God's people, so that our own human perception of the value of various worship forms is not reliable.[12] We must depend on the instructions God provides in His Word. In this case God's command is clear: "Thou shalt not do so" (31*a*). Knowing that people usually want to know why, God provides the explanation. The basic reason for the prohibition is that God does not like pagan worship patterns. Moses

---

[11]Other versions of Deut. 12:31 make this clear: "You shall not worship the Lord your God in that way" (ESV; cf. NIV).

[12]J. A. Thompson observes, "We sense the struggle to lift the worship of Israel from debasing elements. It was clear to Israel's best religious leaders that the mixing of pagan elements with the worship of Yahweh could never lead to a richer faith." *Deuteronomy*, in The Tyndale Old Testament Commentaries, ed. D. J. Wiseman (Downers Grove: InterVarsity, 1974), 172.

uses some strong words to express God's viewpoint: their practices include "every abominable thing that the Lord hates" (31*b*, ESV).

Israel had already encountered some pagan religious practices that they found appealing in the worship of Baal at Peor (Num. 25). This worship featured two main attractions: feasting on food sacrificed to idols and committing sexual immorality with the Midianite women.[13] God's people do not have a very good record when it comes to discerning good among the corrupt aspects of pagan worship; unfortunately, not everything that is abominable in God's eyes is equally repulsive to us. In Deuteronomy 12:31 God identifies one aspect of pagan worship that ought to be disgusting to all: human sacrifice.[14] He presents this extreme example as characteristic of all pagan worship, as if to say, "This is where it leads, so do not start down that path."

Is there a modern parallel to pagan worship that has proven to be a snare to God's people? One particular instance is both surprisingly apparent and yet widely prevalent. In fact, it has become one of the most divisive issues affecting the church today. Until the early 1970s there was a clear distinction between the world and God's people on the issue of rock music. Rock musicians unashamedly identified the purpose for their music: they wanted to communicate their own devotion to sexual immorality, drug and alcohol abuse, and rebellion against authority. Everything about their music

---

[13]Balaam seems to have been the mastermind behind the deceit. The Lord had prevented him from cursing Israel, and Num. 24 closes with Balaam reluctantly leaving Balak, king of Moab, and heading for home. Apparently the lure of Balak's money was too great, though, and Balaam returned with a new plan. Perhaps they could succeed against God's people by enticing them with pagan worship (Num. 31:16). Israel succumbed to the deception, and 24,000 died in the resulting plague. Rev. 2:14 confirms both Balaam's role in the affair as well as the two aspects of pagan worship.

[14]At the lowest points of Israel's history, however, even this found its way into their worship practices. See 2 Kings 16:3 (2 Chron. 28:3); 2 Kings 23:10; Isa. 57:5; Jer. 7:31; 19:5; 32:35; Ezek. 16:20–21; 20:26, 31.

—the lyrics, the musical sounds, even the visual and auditory presentation—they deliberately designed to promote their sinful lifestyle choices. As the years passed, they became increasingly skilled at accomplishing their purpose. Rock music has become one of the primary means by which the world worships the gods of illicit sex, drugs, and rebellion.

Some Christians, noting the widespread popularity of rock music, wondered if it would be possible to incorporate some of the aspects of rock into Christian music. Perhaps that would attract more people to come to church.[15] They decided they had to change one part of rock music. The lyrics were simply too blatantly wicked. The musical sounds and even the performance techniques they retained, arguing that those components are morally neutral. This was the birth of Contemporary Christian Music (CCM), which has dominated church worship music in recent decades.[16] Here, then, is a clear instance in which God's people have succumbed to the very temptation that Deuteronomy 12 has revealed. They have

---

[15]Their calculated effect has largely proven to be correct: both Christians and unsaved people generally seem to be more willing to attend churches that offer CCM. Rick Warren, founding pastor of Saddleback Valley Community Church in Orange County, California, gives this testimony: "Saddleback is unapologetically a contemporary music church. We've often been referred to in the press as 'the flock that likes to rock.' We use the style of music the majority of people in our church listen to on the radio. Years ago, after being frustrated with trying to please everyone, I decided to survey our church. I passed out 3x5 cards to everyone in the crowd service and asked them to write down the call letters of the radio station they listened to. What we discovered is that 96 percent of our people said they listen to middle-of-the-road adult contemporary music.... After surveying who we were reaching, we made the strategic decision to stop singing hymns in our seeker services. Within a year of deciding what would be 'our sound,' Saddleback *exploded* with growth." *The Purpose Driven Church* (Grand Rapids: Zondervan, 1995), 285.

[16]For more information on this important topic, see John Makujina, *Measuring the Music* (Willow Street, PA: Old Paths Publications, 2002); John Blanchard and Dan Lucarini, *Can We Rock the Gospel?* (Webster, NY: Evangelical Press, 2006); Dan Lucarini, *Why I Left the Contemporary Christian Music Movement* (Webster, NY: Evangelical Press, 2002); Frank Garlock and Kurt Woetzel, *Music in the Balance* (Greenville, SC: Majesty Music, 1992) and Tim Fisher, *The Battle for Christian Music*, 2nd ed. (Greenville, SC: Sacred Music Services, 2004).

observed how the world worships its gods and incorporated aspects of that worship into their worship of the Lord. Moreover, no one can argue that this is just an Old Testament principle. Romans 12:2, in another context of worship (presenting a "living sacrifice" to God), issues this specific command: "And be not conformed to this world." The use of CCM is a modern instance of worshiping like the world, an aspect of false worship that God prohibits.

Worship Marketed for Convenience (1 Kings 12:26–31)

Jeroboam, ruler of the newly established Northern Kingdom of Israel, perceived that he was facing a difficult circumstance. On the one hand, the Lord had promised to give Jeroboam the ten northern tribes because Solomon had disobeyed the Lord's commandments, particularly concerning false worship (1 Kings 11:31–33). In addition, God had assured Jeroboam that if he would obey His commands, he would enjoy God's presence during his lifetime and a stable dynasty after his death, similar to that of David (38). On the other hand, Jeroboam was worried about his long-term stability. The Lord had given him ten tribes just as He said, but would He fulfill His other promises? The problem centered on the issue of worship. The temple in Jerusalem was still the only authorized place to worship the Lord, but Jerusalem was the capital of the Southern Kingdom of Judah. If his people continued to go to Jerusalem to worship, Jeroboam reasoned, they might be impressed with all its royal magnificence and decide to return their allegiance to its king. That could mean the end of Jeroboam's reign and possibility the end of his life (12:27). Should he trust the Lord and worship Him the way He says?

Jeroboam decided that he could not trust the Lord to keep His word. In order to protect himself, then, he decided to institute new forms of worship to replace the true worship available in Jerusalem. The result was an odd mixture of truth and falsehood.

First, he disobeyed the prohibition against images by making two golden calves, no doubt following the pattern of false worship at Sinai (28). Then he defied God's command to worship in Jerusalem by placing the calves strategically at Bethel in the south and Dan in the north (29). Next he instituted illegal high places and commissioned non-Levites to serve as priests (31). Finally, he established festivals that deliberately imitated celebrations going on in Jerusalem (32).

He seemed to sense, however, that all this might not be enough. Worship traditions tend to run deep, making people reluctant to accept change. Besides, most of Jeroboam's ideas were unbiblical. How could he convince the people to follow his worship instead of the worship that God had authorized in His Word? It was a difficult challenge, but together with his counselors he devised a plan for success: a marketing strategy for worship. "Whereupon the king took counsel, and made two calves of gold, and said unto them, It is too much for you to go up to Jerusalem: behold thy gods, O Israel, which brought thee up out of the land of Egypt" (28).

This plan has two key parts. First, he focused on convincing the people that this new form of worship was better for them. That was a new concept for God's people. Until this time they had believed that true worship was all about God, what He deserved and desired, and what was best for Him. Here was a worship leader who was taking their personal concerns into account. In particular, he appealed to their sense of convenience.[17] The road to Jerusalem was a challenging journey from anywhere in the Northern Kingdom. Even those living within a few miles (Bethel is about

---

[17]Donald J. Wiseman notes that Jeroboam devised his worship strategy "for reasons of convenience and expediency." *1 and 2 Kings*, in The Tyndale Old Testament Commentaries, ed. D. J. Wiseman (Downers Grove: InterVarsity, 1993), 144.

10 miles from Jerusalem) faced a difficult climb up the mountain (Jerusalem is about 2,300 feet above sea level). For those in the northern sections of the country, the distance extended to as much as 100 miles. The men were required to make that journey three times each year. Jeroboam's plan was simple: if he established two centers for worship in the extreme north and south of his kingdom, everyone would have a significantly easier journey.[18] Jeroboam seems to have understood human nature.

The second part of his plan was also important. These people were sensitive to the dangers involved with worshiping false gods. They had experimented with that at various times in the past, and it never worked out very well for them. Jeroboam would need to convince them that even though the forms of worship were new and different from what God had commanded, they were still worshiping the same God.[19] He identified the golden calves, then, with the God Who had delivered them from Egypt. Jeroboam was reaching all the way back to the founding of the nation and to an event that everyone attributed to the Lord. The worship is different, he was saying, but the God is the same.[20] Apparently his marketing strategy worked. For several centuries after Jeroboam instituted these changes, God's people from the Northern Kingdom worshiped at Bethel and Dan.

---

[18]ESV reflects a slightly different tactic: "You have gone up to Jerusalem long enough" (1 Kings 12:28*b*), suggesting that it was simply time for a change of location. Most other translations, however, agree with the KJV, placing the emphasis on the difficulty of the journey. See the NASB, NIV, NET Bible ("It is too much trouble for you to go up to Jerusalem"), and HCSB ("Going to Jerusalem is too difficult for you").

[19]C. F. Keil offers a paraphrase of Jeroboam's words: "This is no new religion, but this was the form of worship which our fathers used in the desert, with Aaron himself leading the way." "The First Book of Kings," in *Commentary on the Old Testament* (Grand Rapids: Eerdmans, rpt. 1975), 3:198.

[20]The plural *gods* presents the same translational and interpretational challenges here as in Exod. 32, except that here the plural is more appropriate since there were two golden calves. The connection with the deliverance from Egypt, however, is still the deciding factor in favor of a reference to Yahweh. (See the translation in NET Bible.)

What was God's response? Right away, in 1 Kings 12:30, He labeled this worship as sin. Then the next chapter tells about a man of God from Judah whom God sent to prophesy the future destruction of Jeroboam's worship center. Chapter 14 records the prophecy of the destruction of Jeroboam's dynasty and the death of his oldest son. From that point on virtually every king of the Northern Kingdom was assessed negatively at his death because, among other things, he "walked in the way of Jeroboam, and in his sin wherewith he made Israel to sin" (1 Kings 15:34 and many other instances). Israel never recovered from this sin, continuing until the exile recorded in 2 Kings 17. Verses 21–22 of that chapter close a long summary of sins that caused the destruction of Israel, with yet one more reference to the worship Jeroboam instituted:

> For he rent Israel from the house of David; and they made Jeroboam the son of Nebat king: and Jeroboam drave Israel from following the Lord, and made them sin a great sin. For the children of Israel walked in all the sins of Jeroboam which he did; they departed not from them.

A 9th-century-BC marketing strategy that offered convenient worship led God's people in the wrong direction. A 20th-century marketing strategy seems to be following a similar pattern. A newspaper advertisement for a new church in the 1990s offered the following enticements:

> Would you be interested in attending church:
>
> If you could sleep in late on Sunday morning?
>
> If you could wear jeans to church?
>
> If the music was contemporary?
>
> If the message was relevant to life today?
>
> Then come as you are!

This statement comes directly from the church marketing movement.[21] It also reflects the strategy of appealing to people based on personal convenience, with the assumption that worship the way I like it will also be pleasing to God. According to 1 Kings 12, that might not be a good assumption. I have already addressed the issue of contemporary music, and the relevance of sermons has come up in chapter 1. What about a service schedule designed to let people "sleep in late on Sunday"? First, we must acknowledge that there is nothing particularly spiritual about inconvenience; otherwise churches would have their worship services at 3:00 a.m. Furthermore, some churches offer multiple service choices because they do not have adequate space for everyone to worship at the same time. By necessity, then, one service would be earlier or later than another would. The trend in our day, however, seems to be the scheduling of services specifically to cater to the convenience or preferences of people, allowing them to "fit" worship into their busy schedules. Doesn't that imply that other things are more important than worshiping God? Sometimes the "other things" include reading the Sunday newspaper or going to the beach. Ultimately such practices are encouraging the individual to set himself ahead of God, the very opposite of the biblical priority.

Casual dress has been another key feature of the seeker-friendly approach to worship, and it is a challenging issue. On the one hand, dress should not be an obstacle hindering the lost from coming to Christ. In that sense a required dress standard for admittance to a worship service would be wrong. For those who know God, on the other hand, the matter is different. To argue that the clothing

---

[21]For a biblical perspective on the church marketing movement, see David Doran, "Market-Driven Ministry: Blessing or Curse?" in *Detroit Baptist Seminary Journal* 1 (Spring and Fall 1996); and John MacArthur, Jr., *Ashamed of the Gospel: When the Church Becomes Like the World* (Wheaton, IL: Crossway, 1993).

of a worshiper is a non-factor fails to take all the biblical data into account.

The instructions for worship in the tabernacle included what Aaron and his sons should wear while leading in worship. Exodus 28:2 presents the general concept: "And thou shalt make holy garments for Aaron thy brother for glory and for beauty." Of course, there is no corresponding command for lay people, unless you take into account that all believers today are part of a "holy priesthood" (1 Pet. 2:5).[22] Psalm 96:9, though, calls upon all people to "worship the Lord in holy attire" (NASB). Some translations place the emphasis on inner holiness, but H. C. Leupold argues that the phrase refers to "such outward garb and demeanor as befits those that recognize the nature of the God they adore."[23] Holy attire would be clothing that is especially appropriate for those who approach the God of the universe and want to honor Him in every way possible.[24] One way to apply that ideal would be for one to wear the best that he has. That would vary from culture to culture and from one time period to another within a culture. Most cultures, however, have a way of communicating to others that a particular event (in

---

[22]Perhaps God's strategy was to let the leaders set the example, indicating that clothing does matter to God, and let the people draw their own conclusions about what would be appropriate for them to wear. If so, this might provide a good pattern for churches in our day: expect the leaders to set a good example, and let the others follow.

[23]*Exposition of the Psalms* (1959; rpt. Grand Rapids: Baker, 1969), 685. NET Bible also renders this phrase "worship the Lord in holy attire."

[24]Rick Warren, setting the standard for other seeker-friendly churches, has chosen to focus on making unsaved people feel comfortable in the worship service instead of making God feel honored. Here is his approach to Saddleback Sam, his composite profile of the typical unchurched person in his community: "Sam, because he is a southern Californian, prefers casual, informal meetings over anything stiff and formal. He loves to dress down for the mild southern California climate. We take this into account when planning services to attract Sam. For example, I never wear a coat and tie when I speak at Saddleback services. I intentionally dress down to match the mind-set of those I'm trying to reach." *Purpose Driven Church*, 171.

this case a worship service) is important.[25] Those who receive that message would include the Lord Himself as well as other believers, but those who do not know God might also observe what a worshiper is wearing and conclude that his God must be special. It would be another way, then, to "say among the heathen that the Lord reigneth" (Ps. 96:10). If a neighbor observes you leaving your house on a Sunday morning and concludes from your clothing that you might be going to Walmart, you have missed a good opportunity to testify about the greatness of your God. Even more importantly, you have missed an opportunity to tell your God that you think He is important.[26]

---

[25]One way to discern how a particular culture expresses that an event is important would be to observe how most people dress for special occasions such as weddings, funerals, professional appointments, official functions (such as an audience at the White House or Congress), etc. Of course, some people may refuse to submit to such cultural norms, but they are sending a message as well.

[26]Some insist, from 1 Cor. 11:1–16, that women must wear a head covering for worship. Each person must settle this issue for himself, but the following observations might provide help in reaching a decision. *(1) This passage is not about hats*—The head covering in the ancient world was a shawl hanging "down from the head" (a literal rendering of the phrase κατὰ κεφαλῆς ἔχων), hiding the entire head from view. Modern hats are usually much too small and stylish to hide the woman's head at all. In fact, since they are designed to be attractive, they actually draw *more* attention to her head, especially in cultures where hats are not common. *(2) This passage is not about adding something to the head for worship*—In the culture of the ancient world, a respectable woman would cover her head whenever she was in public. Paul was simply urging women to retain their customary cover, not add a special one for worship, thus maintaining their current cultural sensitivities. *(3) This passage is not about a timeless, universal clothing standard*—That head covers are cultural and not inherently right or wrong in worship is evident from the OT: the priests' worship garments included hats (Lev. 8:9, 13), in apparent contradiction to 1 Cor. 11:4. In fact, the Jewish priests continued to lead in worship with their heads covered at the temple in Jerusalem while Paul was writing this letter to believers in Greece. Besides, the only direct command is at the end of vs. 6, and even that is tied to a conditional clause based on a cultural sense of shame. *(4) This passage is not about subordination of women*—The theme is giving glory to God in worship, and Paul's reasoning is precise. In first-century Greek culture, a Christian man worshiping with his physical head uncovered honored his metaphorical head (Christ). A woman worshiping with her physical head uncovered, however, had the exact opposite effect of dishonoring her metaphorical head (her husband). Why? Because a woman's uncovered head brought glory to her husband, which was inappropriate in a worship service where glory belongs to God alone. Ironically, her uncovered

WORSHIPING THE RIGHT WAY WITH THE WRONG HEART

Wrong worship can take many forms, and some may be more difficult to discern than others. Especially subtle are those aspects of wrong worship that appear to be following biblical patterns on the outside. What is going on inside the heart only God knows for sure, but He has included enough examples in Scripture for people to know that He rejects worship when the heart is not right, even when the outward manner might be correct.

Ritual Worship (Genesis 4:1–16)

Some maintain that God rejected Cain because he was offering the wrong kind of sacrifice. God required a slain animal, like the one Abel presented to the Lord, not fruit from the ground. That would place this incident into the previous category of worshiping the right God in the wrong way. Such a perspective, however, ignores the New Testament commentary on this passage, which states that the key feature of Abel's acceptance was his faith in God: "By faith Abel offered unto God a more excellent sacrifice than Cain" (Heb. 11:4). That would imply, of course, that Cain was lacking in faith. Besides, there is no evidence that either brother was offering a sacrifice of atonement. It is more likely that these were acts of worship in which each was presenting to the Lord a portion of his income from his own labor.[27] One was a shepherd, and the other was a farmer. Neither profession was inherently nobler than the other. Indeed, God had commissioned Adam both to work in the garden (Gen. 2:15) and to tend the animals (Gen. 2:19). It is better to conclude that the content of Cain's sacrifice was acceptable; the problem was at a deeper level.

---

head dishonored her husband by pointing to him in a situation where he wanted no such attention. By covering her head, she was able to give honor directly to God.

[27]See John H. Sailhamer, "Genesis," in *The Expositor's Bible Commentary* (Grand Rapids: Zondervan, 1990), 2:61.

The first indication that the problem was in Cain's heart comes in verse 5. When he learned that God had rejected his offering, his response was anger. This is remarkable considering that he was dealing directly with God. Rather than fall to his knees, pleading for mercy and instruction (if he didn't already know what was wrong), he chose to express his rejection of God's requirements for true worship. It is as if he were saying, "You ought to be satisfied, because this is the only kind of worship you deserve." By contrast God is exceedingly gracious, inviting Cain to return through the door of repentance and forgiveness; then all would be well. Even the warning is gracious, informing Cain that if he refuses the safety of a restored relationship with God, the beast of rebellion was lurking nearby, ready to pounce. The only hope for victory over sin is to turn to the Lord (7).

Sadly, Cain made the wrong choice. Falling under the dominance of his own sinful passions, he conspired against his brother and murdered him in the open field. Even then the door of repentance was open, but once again he responded to God's patient inquiries with insolence and denial. As soon as God pronounced his punishment, Cain seemed to sense the implications. In this context, to "be hid" from God's face (14) means more than loss of fellowship; it means that all future attempts to worship would be equally futile. Since worshiping God is man's highest purpose, Cain had lost everything that matters. Still he stubbornly persisted in rebellion, protesting that his punishment was unbearable. All his complaint secured, however, was the guarantee that his misery would continue throughout a normal lifespan (15). Such is the condition of those who refuse to advance beyond mere ritualistic forms of worship, choosing to withhold their heart from God and wander through life alone in a purposeless existence. Right from the beginning God rejected worship that doesn't come from the heart.

Token Worship (1 Samuel 15:1–23)

The defining moment in the career of King Saul came while he was under a specific assignment from the Lord. Samuel had commissioned him to punish the Amalekites for their attack against God's people when Israel had come up from Egypt. The offense had occurred about 400 years earlier, an implicit warning to Saul (and others) that God's punishment of sin may be slow, but it is certain. Saul had already demonstrated that his character was weak concerning obedience and worship (1 Sam. 13:8–14). Here was one more opportunity to submit to the Lord and do what was right. Samuel's instructions were clear: Saul must destroy Amalek, both the people and the livestock (15:3), and there must be no exceptions.

Saul's obedience was immediate, but it was not complete. He destroyed all the people except the king (presumably the "best" person), and he destroyed all the worthless animals but kept the best of the livestock alive. This already reveals a worship deficiency in Saul's life. The word translated "utterly destroy" (KJV, in both v. 3 and v. 9) includes a religious connotation. Saul was to "devote to destruction" (ESV) all that they had. In other words, he must devote them to the Lord by destroying them. There were only two options available: keep the goods for themselves or give them to the Lord. In this case God commanded that they must give everything to Him. The means for accomplishing that was destruction.[28] We can express the spiritual aspect of this destruction a little more explicitly, showing that 1 Samuel 15:9 exposes the heart

---

[28]The noun form of the same word occurs in Josh. 6:17 concerning the destruction of Jericho. Joshua announced to Israel that everything in that city was "devoted to the Lord for destruction" (ESV). In other words, God placed all the material goods under a ban, prohibiting His people from using them for their own purposes. Utter destruction would demonstrate that everything belonged to the Lord. See Richard S. Hess, *Joshua*, in The Tyndale Old Testament Commentaries (Downers Grove: InterVarsity, 1996) 132. In essence, then, Achan stole the silver, gold, and garments directly from

of the problem with a stark contrast: "But Saul and the people spared Agag, and the best of the sheep, and of the oxen, and of the fatlings, and the lambs, and all that was good, and would not [devote them to the Lord]: but every thing that was vile and refuse, that they [devoted to the Lord]." What was wrong with Saul's worship? Deep down, he really wanted the best for himself. He was willing to serve the Lord as long as there was some profit in it for him.

God observed Saul's disobedience and told Samuel all about it. In grief and anger Samuel went out to meet Saul as he returned from the battle, only to hear Saul boast about his complete obedience to God's command. There was one problem, however: Samuel could hear the sounds of live animals. Saul was ready with an excuse and entered the first stage of shifting the blame. The people did it, he explained, adding that he thought the reason was acceptable: they planned to offer sacrifice to the Lord.

There are three possibilities here. First, perhaps Saul planned to offer all the animals he had spared to the Lord as burnt offerings. If so, it was a bad plan. They already belonged to the Lord anyway (devoted to destruction), so why disobey the Lord in order to worship the Lord? This is not likely to be the truth. Second, it could be that he (and the people) planned to keep the animals for themselves and only suggested the sacrifice idea as a last-minute way to get out of a jam. If this option assumes that after Samuel exposed his plan, Saul was willing to sacrifice all the animals to God, it might be true.

Another scenario, however, seems more likely. Saul knew he was disobeying God's command by sparing the animals, but he

---

the Lord (Josh. 7). The goods from all the other cities in the conquest, however, the people could keep for themselves. God must have the first fruits.

91

couldn't bear to see them wasted (on the Lord!). His plan, then, was to keep most of the animals for himself and give some of them to the Lord in a public display of worship. If so, this reveals a serious misconception about worship that is still common today. Some are unwilling to submit to God's Word, considering it too restrictive on their lifestyle. They essentially live for self during the week, doing what pleases them even if that means disobeying the Lord. A twinge of conscience still operates, however, so they must do something to try to alleviate the guilt. The chosen method of relief is worship. Not true worship, of course, because that would require genuine submission. Token worship will have to do. Token worship is the attempt to compensate for sin (which he has still not confessed or forsaken) by giving something to God (perhaps an hour or so on Sunday morning and maybe even some money in the offering plate).

The problem is that God does not accept token worship. He refers to it as disobedience and "evil" (19). Because those who offer such worship really don't understand the problem, they are ready to argue their case. Listen to Saul's insistence (perhaps emphasizing the word *have* in each clause): "I have obeyed the voice of the Lord, and have gone the way which the Lord sent me, and have brought Agag the king of Amalek, and have utterly destroyed the Amalekites" (20). He knows he is claiming too much, however (he just admitted to sparing Agag), so he resorts again to casting the blame on the people (as if the king was helpless), but ultimately he rests his case on the supposed value of his worship (21). Samuel rejects his arguments with a key statement that exposes the foolishness of token worship (22–23):

> And Samuel said, Hath the Lord as great delight in burnt offerings and sacrifices, as in obeying the voice of the Lord? Behold, to obey is better than sacrifice, and to hearken than the fat of rams. For rebellion is as the sin of witch-

craft, and stubbornness is as iniquity and idolatry. Because thou hast rejected the word of the Lord, he hath also rejected thee from being king.

In Saul's case God's rejection was both complete and final. Even Saul's admission of guilt and request for forgiveness did not reverse the effects of his punishment (24–26). The sobering message is that there is a limit to God's patience with token worship and the disobedience it vainly tries to cover. It is best to repent of this wrong worship now while there is still time.

Reluctant Worship (Malachi 1:6–14)

The prophet Malachi was a contemporary with Nehemiah who ministered to the exiles who had returned from Babylon. Through that experience God's people had finally learned to forsake the sin of idolatrous worship of false gods, but they still struggled with worshiping the true God in the right way. Malachi was there to help, exposing what was wrong and exhorting them to change. What he discovered was insincere worship, evident by their reluctant participation in the temple ceremonies. The prophet was not limited to his own observation, however: God provided insight to the inner attitudes of the people toward worship. Malachi often expresses these insights through hypothetical conversations between God and His people, with God quoting statements by the people. It is likely that the people never actually said the things attributed to them, but God knew exactly what they were thinking.[29] Like the previous aspects of wrong worship, this is also a common problem in our day. As long as people are conforming to acceptable outward forms of worship, they suppose that what they are thinking on the inside does not matter. In chapter 1, Malachi

---

[29]See Pieter A. Verhoff, *The Books of Haggai and Malachi*, in The New International Commentary on the Old Testament, ed. R. K. Harrison (Grand Rapids: Eerdmans, 1987), 166.

responds by pointing to the love of God (1–5) and the greatness of God (6–14), insisting that anything less than whole-hearted worship is not good enough for Him.

According to verses 6–8, God deserves true worship. Based on the relationship He sustains with His people as Father/son and Master/servant, He should receive honor and not disdain. His people were showing disdain, however, by giving God less than their best. Gifts that would be unthinkable if offered to a human dignitary might seem good enough to express worship. Even though this passage fits under the heading of worshiping God the right way with the wrong heart, it becomes evident that when the heart attitude is wrong the worship form will not be exactly right either. The people's questions in verses 6 and 7 indicate that it is possible to be guilty of such wrong worship and not even know it.

There are consequences for wrong worship. Verse 9 is full of irony: after offering God such deficient worship, go ahead and try asking for His help. You will find that God senses no obligation to answer your prayers. In fact, He would prefer no worship at all instead of the emptiness of ongoing wrong worship (10). We usually suppose that something is better than nothing, but that is not true about worship. God's perspective is that lack of honor is better than dishonor. Besides, God is looking ahead to the day when He will receive worldwide genuine worship (probably a reference to the millennium in v. 11). He can be patient until then, but He should not have to wait.

The confrontation becomes a little more direct and personal in verses 12–14. With their current worship patterns, God's people profane His name, pollute His table and despise His gifts. These terms are strong enough to indicate that God regards their worship as unacceptable. They probably reflect a critical attitude toward various aspects of the worship services, which did not provide sufficient pleasure to satisfy the worshipers. In fact, the Lord discerns that they are bored with the whole process (13). God's response to their weariness is in stark contrast to the strategy of the church marketing movement. Rather than provide fresh, entertaining elements of worship designed to please people, God calls on people to change their wrong attitude and realize that worship is about pleasing God, not them. By the time of Malachi, the Mosaic worship ceremonies had continued unchanged for almost 1000 years. Apparently God does not need to have variety in order to maintain His interest in worship, and He expects people to conform to His preferences. Boredom with the worship forms that God has ordained is unacceptable to God. A worshiper who constantly checks his watch, wondering why the time is passing so slowly, needs to check his heart instead. That kind of attitude toward worship leads to wrong forms of worship that God rejects, similar to bringing a blemished animal to the temple for sacrifice (13). That would be cheating the Lord out of the worship He deserves as the great King and Lord of hosts, bringing God's curse instead of His blessing (14).

Pretentious Worship (Matthew 15:8–9)

The Gospel accounts portray Jesus Christ coming face to face with wrong worship on numerous occasions, usually in confrontations with the Pharisees. He openly acknowledged that they were meticulous in their observance of the law. At times they went to extremes to make sure they were doing all that God required, including giving God ten percent of their garden herbs (Luke 11:42). In public perception they were the best examples of godliness and piety anyone knew. They tried to honor God, setting an example for others to follow, and worship was no exception. No one could beat the Pharisees when it came to faithfulness at the temple services.

Christ, however, was not impressed. For all their outward conformity, their righteousness was inadequate for entrance into the kingdom of heaven (Matt. 5:20). Even what they did that was right they did for the wrong reason: "But all their works they do for to be seen of men" (23:5). People could see only the outward appearance, but the Lord knew that on the inside they were "full of hypocrisy and iniquity" (28). Christ's catalog of their sins dominates Matthew 23. On one occasion, after identifying the Pharisees as hypocrites, Christ applied the description of Isaiah 29:13 directly to them (Matt. 15:8–9):

> This people draweth nigh unto me with their mouth, and honoureth me with their lips; but their heart is far from me. But in vain they do worship me, teaching for doctrines the commandments of men.

Their approach to God was limited to a verbal profession, which the condition of the heart nullified. The result was that their worship was vain: empty, worthless, without reality, purpose, or intended effect.[30] That is a sad commentary on a common form of wrong worship, whether it occurs in Christ's day or our own.

LOOKING BACK

God's Word contains numerous examples of wrong worship in action. In spite of a wide variety of features, all the instances have three things in common. First, the participants believed that their worship would be acceptable to God. Each one should have known better, because God had revealed what He wanted. Somehow self-deception can be more convincing than divine revelation. The second shared trait is that God rejected each form of wrong worship completely and decisively. Wrong worship is still wrong even if it

---

[30]See the word group under μάταιος in *The Theological Dictionary of the New Testament*, ed. G. Kittel, G. W. Bromiley and G. Friedrich (Grand Rapids: Eerdmans, 1964).

is sincere. When God has spoken, ignorance of His will is not a valid excuse. The third characteristic: each of these ancient forms of wrong worship has a modern counterpart. The practices might have changed, but the same principles continue to deprive God of the honor He deserves. Furthermore, no one can safely assume that his own worship is untainted by wrong traits. Some kinds of wrong worship are blatant, but others are subtle and move into the heart gradually. The biblical record calls upon each worshiper to examine his own worship practices, seeking God's grace to eliminate everything that is false.

CONCLUSION

This study has attempted to explore three important questions. First, the positive side of this issue: what is right worship? The essence of right worship includes a focus on the right person (God alone), the right purpose (giving God glory), and the right pattern (in spirit and truth). Putting those principles into practice requires diligent effort to give God glory through the five elements of true worship. Preparation is necessary both before and after one arrives at the place of worship. Praise demands careful attention both to the manner of the music (how one sings) and the message of the music (what one sings). Prayer is also an effective element of worship, as long as the worshipers follow the biblical pattern and earnestly follow the one leading in prayer. God also expects the worshiper to present his tithes and offerings to the Lord as act of worship. Finally, the preaching of God's Word gives God glory when the worshiper both hears God's voice (through faithful exposition) and responds in submission. All five elements are essential for a complete worship experience that is acceptable to God.

Second, does worship style matter to God? The answer from Scripture is unequivocally affirmative. God's desires and requirements for worship form a relatively narrow set of standards. The so-called "regulative principle" of worship, the concept that worship must follow the guidelines that God has established, is inherently biblical.

God not only reveals in His Word exactly what He expects, He also reveals His response to the worship styles He observes. According to Exodus 20, He punishes wrong worship severely, with grandchildren and great-grandchildren feeling the effects of a father's errant worship practices. The destruction of the families of Dathan and Abiram (Num. 16) provides a grim historical example. On the other hand, God promises blessings that are virtually unlimited to the families of those who commit themselves to giving God right worship. Abraham's obedience to God in Genesis 22 has already brought great blessings on his descendants, and the best is yet to come in the form of the millennial kingdom with Jerusalem as the capital. God has provided sufficient motivation to make worship style as important to us as it is to Him.

The realization that God punishes wrong worship styles makes the third question even more urgent: what is wrong worship? Scripture records two categories of historical instances of wrong worship that reveal the principles behind unacceptable worship styles. The first category portrays people worshiping the right God in the wrong way. God rejects worship when it comes from human imagination about God (Aaron's golden calf), when it is innovative in departing from God's prescribed forms (Nadab and Abihu's strange fire), when it imitates the world (the Canaanites' worship styles), and when it is marketed for convenience (Jeroboam's golden calves). The second category of wrong worship shows people following a right worship style but with the wrong heart attitude. Examples of this failure include ritual worship (Cain's offering), token worship (Saul's sheep), reluctant worship (Malachi's audience), and pretentious worship (the Pharisees). The consequences in each case clearly reveal that all such attempts to honor the Lord are worthless and even harmful.

Unfortunately, in spite of the clarity of His Word, God does not receive the worship He deserves in the way that He demands. This constitutes a serious problem, not only because wrong worship has unpleasant consequences for us, but more importantly because God's glory is our most important function.

The Great Commission, in its two phases, is the direct answer to deficiency in worship (Matt. 28:19–20). First, the Lord deserves more worshipers, so we must make more disciples of Jesus Christ. Second, He deserves better worshipers, so we must continually strive to learn and teach everything He has revealed in His Word to the entire body of disciples, both recent converts and older saints. Doing this will ultimately eliminate the "hesitancy" of worship.

All this highlights the fact that worship is the primary motivation for ministry, whether that ministry focuses on evangelizing the lost or edifying God's people. In fact, it should be the primary motivation for everything we do. Nothing is more important than worship, either now or in eternity.